"And do not pursue that of which you have no knowledge. Indeed, the hearing, the sight, and the heart—about all those [one] will be questioned." (Qur'an, 17:36)

Religious Content in the Age of AI

(Finding a Balance between Ease and Authenticity)

Iftikhar Ahmad

This book is a product of sincere intellectual effort, written with the intent to educate, raise awareness, and promote responsible engagement with religious content in the digital age. All sacred texts referenced are cited respectfully and in accordance with common academic and interfaith standards.

Cover design by Iftikhar Ahmad

First Edition: 2025

Disclaimer

This book is a work of academic inquiry and reflective exploration. It is intended solely for educational, ethical, and intellectual engagement. The author does not represent, nor claim to speak on behalf of, any official religious institution, theological council, or technological organization.

All religious references, quotations, and discussions are presented in good faith, based on publicly available sources and widely accepted interpretations. Readers are encouraged to consult qualified scholars, authentic religious authorities, and primary source material when making theological decisions or seeking spiritual guidance.

The perspectives expressed herein are the result of extensive and objective research and do not necessarily reflect the views of any specific religious denomination, school of thought, or technology provider.

Any references to AI platforms, tools, or companies are used strictly for illustrative and explanatory purposes, and do not imply endorsement, critique, or affiliation beyond their relevance to the book's educational goals.

Dedication

This book is dedicated first and foremost to **all the Prophets** who have guided humanity through divine wisdom — **especially Prophet Muhammad (PBUH)**, the pinnacle and crown of them all, whose teachings remain a beacon of truth and enlightenment.

To the **founders of all true religions** who have laid the foundations of divine guidance for the betterment of humanity, inspiring generations to seek knowledge and righteousness.

And to the **unsung heroes** — the scholars, preservers, and seekers of truth — who have dedicated their lives to safeguarding this sacred knowledge, ensuring its continuity through the ages. Humanity will forever owe its spiritual growth and understanding to their tireless efforts.

For, as **religious and spiritual wisdom** aligns with the **advancement of human society**, they are the soul and the body — inseparable and complementary, each making the other whole.

Table of Contents

Preface

In today's world, where information is at our fingertips and technology evolves at an unprecedented pace, the question of authenticity has never been more crucial. As artificial intelligence reshapes how we access and interact with knowledge, it brings both convenience and a profound responsibility. From academic research to daily news, AI can process vast amounts of information, but can it truly verify the depth, context, and truth of what it delivers? This question of authenticity—whether in news, history, or general knowledge—poses a challenge that we must navigate carefully.

Nowhere is this concern more critical than in the realm of religious content. Sacred teachings, passed down through generations, are central to shaping the beliefs, values, and practices of billions of people around the world. But as AI begins to engage with and generate religious content, a pressing dilemma arises: Can machines understand and respect the sanctity of these profound teachings? Can algorithms accurately reflect the wisdom embedded in sacred texts, or do they risk distorting the very essence of what is sacred?

This book was born not from fear of technology, but from a responsibility to question its unchecked influence—especially in areas where authenticity and reverence are paramount. The integration of AI in spiritual guidance raises fundamental concerns: Can a machine comprehend the soul's needs? Can it interpret complex religious contexts that require human insight and empathy?

As a researcher, a student of religion, and an observer of this rapidly changing world, I felt a deep obligation to explore this intersection—not just for scholars and technologists, but for anyone who values truth, integrity, and the preservation of sacred knowledge. My aim is not to oppose technological progress but to ensure that it proceeds with an unwavering commitment to authenticity and respect for the timeless wisdom that has shaped humanity's spiritual journey.

This book is not a technical manual, nor is it confined to any single religious tradition. It is a call—a universal call—to approach sacred knowledge with caution in the digital age. Written for thinkers, seekers, believers, and creators alike, it invites reflection on how we balance the conveniences of technology with the preservation of authenticity and reverence in what we hold most sacred.

May this work serve as a reminder that while artificial intelligence can replicate words, it cannot replicate the depth of human wisdom. And as innovation accelerates, it is the human heart that must remain the final judge of what is true, sacred, and worth preserving.

Iftikhar Ahmad

Acknowledgments

All praise and gratitude are due to **Allah**, the Most Merciful, whose divine guidance, boundless wisdom, and abundant blessings have made the creation of this book possible. It is through His grace that this work has come to life, and I remain deeply grateful for His continual support.

I extend my sincerest thanks to my family, whose unwavering belief in me has been a constant source of strength and motivation throughout this journey. Their love, patience, and encouragement have formed the foundation upon which this book stands.

I am also profoundly thankful to the **teachers, mentors, and friends** who have shared their knowledge and provided invaluable insights.

A special note of appreciation is due to all the **spiritual leaders, scholars, and religious guides** from various traditions who have devoted their lives to preserving the sacred knowledge of our shared humanity. Their tireless efforts in upholding truth and authenticity have shaped this book's content and direction.

I also wish to extend sincere appreciation to the developers, engineers, and visionaries behind the evolution of Artificial Intelligence. While this book addresses the critical need for caution in religious contexts, the broader contributions of AI to humanity — in medicine, education, communication, and accessibility — are truly remarkable.

Finally, I am deeply grateful to everyone who has contributed — whether through their encouragement, feedback, or shared experiences — as this work is the result of a collective effort. I remain forever indebted to those who have made it possible.

Iftikhar Ahmad

Introduction

Imagine, for a moment, if the words you hold dear — the sacred verses you recite, reflect upon, and pass down to future generations — were influenced by something other than human intention. What if these spiritual truths, which have traditionally required careful study, reverence, and transmission through trusted voices, were now shaped by algorithms — sometimes accurate, but at other times, potentially misleading?

We are living in a time of rapid technological evolution, where Artificial Intelligence, once limited to performing calculations and industrial tasks, is now encroaching upon realms of meaning, language, and even spirituality. It can quote scriptures, offer religious interpretations, and answer profound spiritual questions — all in a matter of seconds. To an untrained eye, these outputs may seem not only correct but authoritative.

However, herein lies the challenge: AI, for all its capabilities, lacks the depth of understanding that comes with human experience. It cannot grasp the sacredness of what it conveys, nor does it possess the reverence required to handle matters of the soul. AI is only as reliable as the data it is trained on, and that data can contain inaccuracies, distortions, or even outright falsehoods. Yet, more and more, people are turning to these tools for spiritual guidance.

This book is not a critique of Artificial Intelligence. Rather, it is a call for caution, responsibility, and awareness—across faiths, cultures, and disciplines. It is written for anyone who values spiritual truth—whether Muslim, Christian, Jewish, Hindu, Buddhist, or anyone seeking wisdom. The challenge at hand is not simply technological or religious. It is a deeply human issue.

The Sacred and the Synthetic — A Fragile Balance

For centuries, religious knowledge has been transmitted with great care and precision. Prophets, saints, scholars, and sages carried the torch of divine wisdom—through oral teachings, written texts, and personal example. Systems of verification, scholarly scrutiny, and spiritual training ensured the integrity of what was passed down. Knowledge was never just information; it was illumination.

Today, that slow, deliberate process is being overshadowed by algorithms designed to predict patterns, not preserve meaning. These tools do not distinguish between truth and error, authentic and fabricated. A verse misquoted, a hadith inaccurately generated, or a religious judgment made without proper context—these occurrences are happening daily, across platforms. And what is concerning is that we are increasingly trusting them, often without realizing the risks involved.

Why This Book Matters — And Why Right Now!

If left unchecked, AI-generated religious misinformation could alter not only individual beliefs but the very fabric of communities. It could lead to:

- Doctrinal confusion among the young and those seeking spiritual answers
- Erosion of trust in religious institutions
- Misinformed actions based on faulty interpretations
- The manipulation of faith for political, ideological, or commercial purposes

This is not a distant threat. It is already happening, and the consequences are real. We cannot afford to be passive observers.

This book aims to be both a wake-up call and a roadmap. It will explore:

- How religious knowledge was traditionally preserved across civilizations
- What AI is, how it functions, and why it falls short in religious contexts
- The theological, psychological, and societal implications of trusting AI with matters of faith
- How we, as individuals, scholars, developers, and communities, can responsibly use technology without compromising the integrity of our spiritual traditions

It brings together insights from theologians, AI researchers, psychologists, historians, and educators—each adding valuable perspectives to this shared human responsibility.

A Universal Concern, A Collective Responsibility

Whether you are a rabbi in New York, an imam in Jakarta, a priest in Rome, a monk in Bangkok, or a tech developer in Silicon Valley—the question remains the same: Can we trust machines with the sacred?

Every faith tradition—from the Abrahamic to the Dharmic—considers divine knowledge a sacred trust, one that should not be taken lightly. And every honest technologist knows: machines are only tools. They can manipulate what we give them, but when misused, they can distort what is most precious.

We must take an active role in protecting the sanctity of sacred knowledge. We are not passive consumers of machine-generated content; we are responsible stewards of what has been passed down to us.

What This Book Promises

By the end of this book, you will:

- Understand the true power and limitations of AI in the realm of religious knowledge

- Be equipped to identify and address AI-generated misinformation
- Gain insights into the history, theology, and technology that protect the integrity of faith
- Learn practical steps to use AI responsibly in both personal and communal religious contexts

This is not a rejection of innovation, but a plea for wisdom, responsibility, and accountability. What is sacred must never be automated without care.

As you read on, remember: this is not just a book. It is a mirror. It reflects our choices—both as individuals and as a species—at a defining moment in history.

Let us move forward with clarity, guided by our values and understanding, ready to meet the challenges ahead with wisdom and a collective commitment to safeguarding the sacred.

Chapter 1: Rediscovering Religious Knowledge in a Digital World

1.1 The Decline of Traditional Learning

The Reverence and Process of Traditional Religious Knowledge Transmission

The transmission of religious knowledge has historically been a highly revered and methodical process. For centuries, religious scholars and teachers have passed down sacred teachings through oral traditions, written texts, and scholarly debates. The classroom was often the religious center, and the teacher was someone with years of scholarly training. Religious knowledge was not simply a matter of memorization; it involved understanding, contemplation, and interpretation—skills honed over time through engagement with mentors and texts. This approach allowed for a deep, authentic connection with religious knowledge.

Challenges in the Digital Age

However, in the digital age, traditional learning methods are facing significant challenges. As the internet expands, it provides immediate access to vast amounts of information, including religious texts, interpretations, and teachings. While this development has its merits—making religious knowledge more accessible than ever—it has also contributed to a decline in the depth and quality of that knowledge. The convenience of searching for answers online has led many to bypass more rigorous learning processes in favor of easily accessible content that may or may not be accurate.

The Erosion of Deep Religious Education

This decline in traditional learning is especially evident in religious education. For example, in the past, students would engage in long-term study of religious texts under the guidance of well-established scholars. This was not a passive experience. The student would ask questions, challenge interpretations, and debate various viewpoints with peers and teachers. Today, many religious discussions are confined to brief online articles, videos, and forums. The time spent deeply analyzing religious teachings has been replaced with quick summaries and sound bites, often produced without sufficient context or scholarly rigor.

The Role of Unqualified Sources in the Digital Age

Furthermore, the digital age has introduced a proliferation of information from unqualified sources. Everyone with an internet connection now has the ability to publish content—whether through blogs, social media posts, or videos. This democratization of information is beneficial in many ways, but it also means that people can access unverified or misinterpreted religious content just as easily as they can access accurate teachings. A tweet, for instance, can go viral, spreading a simple but potentially flawed interpretation of religious scripture far and wide before it can be corrected by experts.

The Dilution of Religious Knowledge

While digital platforms offer unprecedented convenience, they also facilitate a dangerous trend: the dilution of religious knowledge. For many, the perceived ease of finding answers online means there is less incentive to study the teachings of scholars, participate in religious communities, or engage in deep theological reflection. As more people turn to digital sources for answers, traditional learning methods become less prioritized, leading to an erosion of the depth and authenticity of religious knowledge.

The Long-Term Impact on Faith and Religious Practice

In light of this decline, it is important to assess the long-term impact of this shift on faith and religious practice. While digital resources are invaluable for quick access and convenience, they cannot replace the profound and nuanced understanding that comes from years of study under the guidance of scholars. The reliance on online platforms risks oversimplifying complex religious concepts, ultimately diminishing the richness of religious thought and practice.

The Need to Balance Traditional and Digital Approaches

Thus, as the digital age progresses, we face an urgent need to preserve and nurture the traditional methods of religious learning, ensuring that they are not overshadowed by the convenience and immediacy of digital content. But even as we advocate for a return to traditional methods, we must also recognize the role of digital tools in making religious knowledge more accessible. The challenge lies not in rejecting these modern advancements but in balancing them with the time-honored practices that have sustained religious scholarship for generations.

The Impact of Artificial Intelligence on Religious Knowledge

This issue becomes even more pressing when we consider the potential impact of Artificial Intelligence (AI). While AI has the capacity to enhance access to religious knowledge, its role in the transmission of such knowledge—especially in the absence of traditional checks and balances—can pose significant risks. This will be explored in the next sections, but it is essential to first acknowledge the decline of traditional learning and its implications for the authenticity of religious knowledge in the digital era.

1.2 Sacred Knowledge and Its Impact on Faith and Society

The Evolution of Knowledge in the Digital Age

In a rapidly changing world, where technology has become deeply integrated into every facet of our lives, the very nature of knowledge—and how it is disseminated—has evolved in ways we could scarcely have imagined a few decades ago. Whether religious, scientific, or cultural, knowledge has always been the cornerstone of civilization. It shapes societies, influences individual behavior, and guides ethical frameworks that govern how we interact with one another and with the environment. But in today's digital age, a new challenge has arisen: how can we preserve the authenticity of knowledge in a world overwhelmed by digital content, automated algorithms, and AI-driven systems?

The Impact of Misinformation on Sacred Knowledge

The impact of misinformation has never been so far-reaching. From health advice to political opinions, the reliability of the information we encounter daily is increasingly under scrutiny. Yet, when it comes to sacred knowledge, which carries not only intellectual but profound spiritual significance, the consequences of distortion or misinterpretation are even more dire. Across the globe, countless people look to sacred texts, philosophical teachings, and ethical codes to navigate life, to shape their moral compass, and to find purpose in an otherwise uncertain world. The loss of authenticity in such sources can have a deep impact on society.

Religious Knowledge and Its Role in Society

Religious knowledge, particularly that found in the world's major faith traditions, plays a critical role in shaping individual and collective beliefs. In many parts of the world, sacred texts form the bedrock of society's moral and ethical principles. In Islam, for example, the Qur'an and Hadith guide the hearts and minds of billions of people. But religious knowledge, though powerful, is not isolated from the broader flow of human understanding. It interacts with and is influenced by science, culture, philosophy, and, increasingly, technology.

The Democratization of Knowledge: Blessing or Curse?

Historically, knowledge—sacred or secular—was passed down through generations via scholars, teachers, and community leaders. But in today's hyper-connected world, access to information is at the fingertips of virtually anyone with an internet connection. This unprecedented access to information has opened up both opportunities and challenges. The democratization of knowledge is, in many ways, a blessing. It allows people from all walks of life to engage with ideas, religious teachings, and academic insights that were previously inaccessible. However, with this opportunity comes the danger of misinformation.

The Age of Information Overload

The internet has given rise to an era of "information overload," where people are constantly bombarded with content from countless sources. While much of this information is valuable, a significant amount is inaccurate, misleading, or outright false. This is especially true when it comes to religious knowledge, where inaccurate interpretations of sacred texts, misquotes, and unqualified opinions can quickly gain traction online.

Consequences of Misinformation in Religious Contexts

The consequences of misinformation in the digital age are far-reaching, particularly when it concerns beliefs and practices that govern personal and collective behavior. When religious teachings are misquoted or distorted, the consequences can be spiritually and socially destructive. A misinterpretation of sacred teachings may lead to misguided beliefs, the spread of harmful ideologies, or even violent extremism. The erosion of trust in religious authority, and the weakening of community bonds that often come with a shared understanding of sacred texts, further exacerbates the problem.

Distortion of Knowledge in the Digital Era

This challenge extends beyond religious knowledge. All forms of knowledge—scientific, cultural, and historical—are vulnerable to distortion in a digital world where algorithms often prioritize sensationalism and popularity over accuracy and truth. The rise of "fake news," echo chambers, and algorithm-driven filter bubbles has made it increasingly difficult for individuals to distinguish between truth and falsehood.

The Role of AI in Distorting Knowledge

Therefore, as much as we need to focus on the preservation of religious knowledge, we must also broaden our concern to the integrity of all knowledge in the digital age. The proliferation of AI-generated content—whether in the form of articles, videos, or social media posts—has further complicated the situation. While AI holds immense potential for positive contributions to society, such as aiding in medical research, improving accessibility, and offering personalized learning, it also carries significant risks. AI systems, driven by algorithms that optimize for efficiency rather than truth, can inadvertently distort facts, misinterpret religious texts, or present biased information.

A Global Responsibility for Knowledge Integrity

This issue is not limited to any one faith or belief system. It affects all individuals, regardless of their religious or cultural background. In an increasingly secular world, the same concerns over the integrity of knowledge apply to all fields: from education to science, from the arts to politics. Therefore, the conversation about the authenticity of knowledge—particularly in the context of AI and digital misinformation—must be a global one, involving people from all walks of life.

The Importance of Verifying Information

As we move forward in this new digital age, it is essential that we recognize the importance of verifying information, questioning sources, and ensuring that the knowledge we engage with—whether sacred or secular—is accurate, trustworthy, and authentic. This is not only a religious duty for those who follow sacred texts but also a societal responsibility for all individuals who seek to live a life of truth, integrity, and moral clarity. Only by ensuring the authenticity of knowledge can we hope to preserve the values that form the foundation of our societies and cultures.

1.3 The Growing Misinformation Problem

The Age of Misinformation: A Pervasive Challenge

In our hyper-connected world, misinformation has emerged as one of the most disruptive forces of the digital age. It seeps into every sphere of life—politics, health, history, and most critically, religion. What was once a concern limited to fringe outlets has now become a mainstream crisis. In the realm of religious belief, where clarity and authenticity are paramount, the spread of falsehood is not just a mistake—it is a distortion of sacred truth.

What Is Misinformation and Why Does It Matter?

Misinformation refers to inaccurate or misleading content shared without proper verification, whether intentionally or not. It becomes dangerous when it influences how people understand foundational aspects of their faith. Unlike misinformation in other domains, errors in religious knowledge can alter belief systems, distort ethical values, and fracture communities. When a false quote or misinterpreted verse circulates as truth, it doesn't just confuse individuals—it reshapes their worldview.

The Role of Technology in Distorting Truth

While the internet and AI have revolutionized access to knowledge, they have simultaneously weakened the filters that once protected religious understanding. Previously, knowledge passed through rigorous scholarly chains—sanad, ijazah, peer review, and formal education. Today, those checks are often bypassed. Social media, blogs, and AI tools now function as "religious authorities" in the eyes of millions. This shift has enabled the rapid spread of religious misinformation, sometimes shared by well-meaning individuals unaware of the inaccuracies they perpetuate.

The Rise of Religious Confusion and Misinterpretation

This digital flood of unverified content has created a generation of believers who are overwhelmed, skeptical, and often misinformed. Misquotes of prophetic sayings, decontextualized Quranic verses, and fabricated narrations are widely circulated as authentic. The result? Confusion about basic tenets, widespread theological disputes, and the rise of pseudo-scholars whose credentials lie in popularity rather than knowledge. This confusion doesn't only affect individuals—it fragments communities and fosters spiritual uncertainty.

When AI Gets Religion Wrong

AI-generated religious content adds another layer to the problem. While powerful, AI lacks a soul—it cannot grasp sacred context or divine nuance. A language model might assemble scripture or spiritual teachings based on probability, not understanding. Worse, it may borrow from corrupted sources, outdated translations, or polemical interpretations that distort a religion's core message. For example, an AI might misattribute a statement to the Prophet Muhammad (PBUH), misquote Jesus (peace be upon him), or combine verses from different parts of a sacred text to create a meaning that never existed in tradition. These mistakes aren't just technical—they can have theological, social, and emotional consequences.

Invisible Biases, Visible Consequences

The core issue lies in training data. AI systems learn from what they're fed—and if that data contains distortions, bias, or sectarian slants, those same errors are replicated and magnified. In religious discourse, this can be especially damaging. A subtle misrepresentation of a verse on gender roles, for instance, could shape global perceptions of Islam. The consequences range from internalized guilt among believers to externalized hatred and discrimination.

The Urgency of Safeguarding Sacred Knowledge

This growing crisis calls for more than casual concern. Just as counterfeit currency undermines economies, counterfeit knowledge corrupts faith. Safeguarding religious knowledge in the AI age requires robust systems of verification that combine timeless principles with contemporary tools. Traditional methods—such as scholarly chains of narration and peer-reviewed commentary—must now be adapted to monitor digital content, especially that generated by machines. We need to shift from passively consuming content to actively validating it.

Misinformation and the Fracturing of Trust

The deeper danger lies in what misinformation erodes: **TRUST**. Trust in scripture, in religious leadership, in institutions, and even in one's personal understanding. When every opinion is framed as a valid interpretation and every source is seen as equal, a fog of confusion descends. People begin to question long-standing truths or cling to emotionally appealing falsehoods. This fragmentation weakens the spiritual and social unity that religion is meant to foster.

Moving Toward a Culture of Verification

Yet there is a way forward. It begins with creating a culture where verification is not an afterthought but a shared ethic. Individuals must cultivate critical thinking, consult qualified scholars, and cross-check sources before accepting any religious claim—especially when derived from AI or online platforms. Technologists, too, must take responsibility for building systems that flag unverified religious content and guide users to authentic repositories of knowledge.

The Collective Responsibility of Believers and Builders

In this age, the responsibility lies not only with scholars or engineers—it lies with all of us. We must become conscious curators of what we read, believe, and share. In doing so, we preserve not just the truth, but the integrity of faith itself. Our digital footprints are not trivial; they echo across algorithms and shape the future understanding of religion for generations to come. To guard the sacred, we must commit to truth—even when it's inconvenient, and especially when it's easy to ignore.

1.4 Why Authenticity Matters Now More Than Ever

In a world overflowing with information yet starving for truth, the need for authenticity—particularly in religious knowledge—has never been more urgent. As artificial intelligence (AI) rapidly becomes a primary source of information, the lines between what is accurate and what is algorithmically generated blur. This creates a high-stakes challenge: How do we preserve the sanctity and reliability of divine knowledge in an era dominated by speed, convenience, and artificial intelligence?

This chapter explores why authenticity matters now more than ever—not just for believers or religious scholars—but for society at large, as misinformation and misinterpretation threaten the very foundations of human values, ethical decision-making, and collective spirituality.

A Historical Standard: Sacred Knowledge Was Always Guarded

Throughout history, religious knowledge was protected, verified, and passed on with painstaking care. The scribes of ancient texts, Islamic scholars preserving hadith, Christian theologians copying the Bible, and Buddhist monks memorizing oral traditions—each acted as custodians of truth. Authenticity was not just a preference; it was a sacred obligation.

Take for instance the Islamic tradition of isnād (chain of narration). Before a hadith was accepted, scholars examined the integrity and memory of each narrator and the continuity of the chain—an unparalleled system of authentication. Similarly, in Judaism, the Masoretes ensured that every letter of the Torah was transcribed with such precision that any variation led to the scroll being discarded.

Compare this to the digital age, where anyone—human or machine—can upload a "religious quote" or commentary without scrutiny, and it can go viral within minutes. The guardianship of knowledge has shifted from qualified scholarship to unverified digital noise.

The AI Paradox: Power Without Understanding

Artificial intelligence is powerful—but power without understanding is dangerous. AI systems can process billions of words and generate convincing religious explanations. But does it understand holiness? Nuance? Context? No.

Let's clarify something: AI is not inherently malicious. It does not intend to misguide. It is a tool without soul or conscience. But therein lies the danger. It may confidently quote scripture—but if the source text it pulls from is inaccurate or the context is lost, it produces an error in the name of authority.

Example: Ask an AI tool for a verse about mercy in the Qur'an, and it might provide a fabricated or out-of-context verse due to prior misinformation in its training data. This can mislead the seeker—who trusts the machine more than a fallible human—and unknowingly pass on distorted knowledge to others.

Why Authenticity in Religious Content Is Crucial Today

The stakes are higher than ever because of three interconnected shifts:

- **The Globalization of Information**

People across continents can access religious teachings in seconds. While this is a blessing, it also means a mistake is not local—it's global. A single AI-generated misquote can be translated, reposted, and accepted by millions.

- **The Erosion of Scholarly Authority**

As more people turn to digital platforms and AI for religious knowledge, the traditional role of scholars, teachers, and clergy is being bypassed. This creates a vacuum where unchecked information reigns.

- **Cognitive Biases and Emotional Triggers**

AI often optimizes for engagement, not accuracy. It may generate emotionally resonant but inaccurate statements that go viral. People are more likely to believe and share what aligns with their emotions or existing biases, especially in religious contexts.

Result: The public increasingly consumes content that feels right rather than content that is right.

What Happens When Authenticity Is Lost?

Let's imagine a few consequences when authenticity in religious knowledge is no longer prioritized:

- **Spiritual Confusion:** Misrepresented teachings can lead individuals to lose faith or adopt distorted understandings of their religion.
- **Sectarian Conflict:** Inaccurate interpretations can fuel divisions between sects or religions.
- **Cultural Erosion:** Religions form the backbone of many cultures. When their knowledge base is diluted, so too are cultural values, rituals, and traditions.
- **Moral Ambiguity:** Religious teachings often shape ethical decisions. A misinterpreted rule can lead to **harmful actions justified by corrupted knowledge**.

What Experts Are Warning Us

AI Pioneers:

Dr. Timnit Gebru, former co-lead of Google's Ethical AI team, warned in her research that large language models can produce "fluent nonsense." Their credibility is mistaken for truth. The problem is magnified when applied to religious content.

Sam Altman, CEO of OpenAI, stated, "People will increasingly turn to AI for advice about religion, relationships, and ethics. This is both exciting and terrifying."

Religious Scholars

- Shaykh Hamza Yusuf commented, "We must not outsource our search for truth to machines. Sacred knowledge must pass through human hearts."
- Rabbi Jonathan Sacks (z"l) once said, "Technology gives us power, but only wisdom can give us direction."

A Spiritual Wake-Up Call

Authenticity in religious knowledge is not a luxury. It is a necessity for:

- Preserving truth
- Protecting the minds and souls of the next generation
- Maintaining peace and cohesion in a diverse world

In an age of speed, shortcuts, and artificial intelligence, the temptation to accept information at face value is strong. But truth takes time. Authenticity demands effort.

What Can Be Done? A Preview of What Follows

This book does not merely diagnose the problem. The chapters ahead will present practical, scalable, and faith-rooted solutions to preserve authenticity:

- Training AI with verified religious databases
- Human-AI collaboration in sensitive domains
- Verification tools for the public
- The revival of scholarly engagement in digital spaces

Authenticity is not just the responsibility of developers or religious institutions. It's a moral duty for every user of digital content.

Final Reflection

In a time when digital misinformation can masquerade as divine wisdom, we must become guardians of truth, not just consumers of content.

Authenticity matters because faith matters. Humanity matters. Truth matters. And as we stand at the crossroads of technology and spirituality, we are called not to reject the future—but to navigate it with discernment, responsibility, and reverence.

Chapter 2: Interplay of Algorithms and Divine Knowledge

2.1 What Is AI and How Does It Work?

Artificial Intelligence (AI) has evolved rapidly over the past few decades, emerging as a powerful tool that is reshaping industries and society at large. From autonomous vehicles to virtual assistants, AI is everywhere, but its potential impact is most profound in fields where human decision-making is central — particularly in the realm of knowledge dissemination, including religious content.

Understanding AI requires a blend of technological insight and philosophical contemplation. It is important to demystify AI by examining how it operates and how it is shaping our present and future. In this section, we will explore the foundational principles behind AI, its mechanisms, and its evolution.

Defining AI: The Basics

At its core, AI refers to the ability of machines or software systems to mimic human intelligence. While it's often associated with complex algorithms and robotic systems, AI can be found in simpler forms like machine learning models used for recommendation systems or automated customer service bots.

AI works by analyzing large volumes of data to recognize patterns, make predictions, and perform tasks without human intervention. These tasks range from understanding spoken language (speech recognition) to visual identification (image recognition), and even more advanced cognitive functions like decision-making.

The field of AI can be divided into two primary categories:

- **Narrow AI**: AI that is designed and trained to perform a specific task or set of tasks. This includes systems like Google's search engine or Netflix's recommendation engine. These systems excel in their designated function but are limited in scope.

- **General AI**: A form of AI that could theoretically perform any intellectual task that a human being can. This level of AI is still theoretical and is the subject of ongoing research.

In religious contexts, AI primarily operates within the realm of **narrow AI**, where it processes vast amounts of religious texts and produces content based on programmed algorithms.

How Does AI Work? The Mechanisms Behind AI Systems

AI relies heavily on **machine learning (ML)** and **deep learning (DL)** algorithms to process data. Machine learning is a subset of AI where systems are trained using data to improve their performance over time. Let's break down how AI systems are typically built:

- **Data Collection and Preparation**: AI systems start by gathering large datasets, which could include text, images, or audio. In the case of religious content, AI systems might collect data from thousands of religious texts, lectures, articles, and other forms of media.

- **Training the Model**: Once the data is prepared, AI systems use algorithms to recognize patterns. For instance, a natural language processing (NLP) model might be trained on a dataset of religious texts to learn the language, structure, and context of religious discourse. During training, the AI "learns" the relationships between words, concepts, and ideas.

- **Making Predictions or Decisions**: After training, the AI can then make predictions based on new, unseen data. For example, an AI system could be used to generate new religious content by analyzing patterns from the training dataset and predicting what the next most likely sequence of words would be, given the context.

- **Improvement Through Feedback**: As the AI is exposed to more data and receives feedback (either manually or automatically), it can improve its performance. This is why AI-powered systems like chatbots or content generators can improve over time — the more they are used, the better they get at predicting accurate and relevant responses.

Types of AI Algorithms Relevant to Religious Content Creation

In the context of religious content, several AI algorithms can be employed to process, generate, or recommend materials. Some of the key AI techniques that are commonly used include:

- **Natural Language Processing (NLP)**: NLP allows AI systems to understand, interpret, and generate human language. In religious knowledge contexts, NLP can be used to analyze religious texts, translate them, or even summarize them for a broader audience. This is one of the most critical algorithms for AI when working with religious content.
- **Deep Learning**: Deep learning, a subset of machine learning, is used to model data through layers of neural networks. This can help AI systems understand complex relationships within texts — for example, recognizing themes, historical context, or nuances that are often present in sacred scriptures. Deep learning is particularly relevant for tasks such as image recognition (e.g., recognizing images related to religious events) and audio-to-text transcription (e.g., converting sermons into text).
- **Recommendation Systems**: AI-powered recommendation systems analyze user behavior and suggest content based on patterns observed in vast data sets. In the realm of religious content, these systems can recommend sermons, articles, or even specific verses from religious texts, based on the user's preferences or previous activity.

AI's Evolution: From Tools to Partners in Knowledge Creation

AI has evolved from basic algorithms that merely perform specific tasks to more sophisticated systems capable of generating new content. In the past, AI was primarily used for repetitive, structured tasks. Today, it is advancing into creative fields, including the generation of religious discourse.

However, while AI has made significant progress in content creation, it is still fundamentally limited. AI does not possess understanding or consciousness like a human being. It simply processes data and produces results based on patterns it has been trained to recognize. This lack of true comprehension presents risks, particularly when it comes to religious content, where accuracy and context are paramount.

The Role of AI in Religious Content: The Good, the Bad, and the Ugly

While AI can enhance the accessibility of religious knowledge, it also presents challenges that must be addressed. Here are some benefits and concerns:

Benefits:

- **Accessibility**: AI can make religious knowledge available to a broader audience by providing automated translations, summaries, and recommendations.
- **Efficiency**: AI-powered tools can help scholars, researchers, and practitioners quickly analyze vast amounts of religious texts, providing insights that might otherwise take years of study.

Concerns:

- **Loss of Context**: AI systems, despite their capabilities, cannot grasp the nuances, deep historical context, or spiritual significance inherent in religious texts.

- **Risk of Misinformation**: As AI generates and disseminates content, there is a risk that religious teachings may be distorted or misquoted, especially when dealing with complex or deeply philosophical texts.

Conclusion: What We Need to Know

AI has become an invaluable tool in many sectors, including content creation and knowledge dissemination. However, its application in religious contexts requires careful attention to ensure that sacred knowledge is preserved with integrity. As AI continues to evolve, it is essential to understand its limitations, acknowledge the risks, and take steps to ensure that technology serves humanity in a responsible, ethical manner.

2.2 The Role of AI in Content Creation

Artificial intelligence has emerged as an incredibly powerful tool in the realm of content creation. From text generation to image manipulation and even music composition, AI is increasingly being used to produce high-quality content across various mediums. However, its role in content creation, particularly in fields like religious knowledge, raises important ethical, practical, and philosophical concerns.

A New Era in Content Generation

AI-driven systems have revolutionized how we produce and consume information. Whether it's generating articles, crafting marketing messages, or writing entire books, AI has proven itself to be a remarkably efficient content creator. Technologies like OpenAI's GPT-3 and GPT-4, Google's BERT, Anthropic's Claude, and other advanced natural language processing systems, including models developed by Meta, Microsoft, and smaller research groups, are capable of generating text that is often indistinguishable from that written by humans—sometimes even surpassing it in coherence and grammatical precision.

For instance, AI can now generate articles based on a brief prompt, produce entire chapters of books, and provide detailed explanations of complex topics with a degree of accuracy that was previously unimaginable. This level of productivity is not only transforming traditional content creation but is also creating new opportunities in sectors such as journalism, entertainment, marketing, and yes, even religious discourse.

The Rise of AI in Religious Content Creation

Religious content creation is no exception to this trend. Increasingly, AI is being used to generate religious articles, translations of sacred texts, sermons, and even personalized guidance for spiritual matters. For example, AI-powered tools can summarize religious teachings or generate Quranic translations with context-based adjustments, aiming to make them more accessible to a modern audience. In this sense, AI has the potential to democratize access to religious knowledge, making it available to people who may not have the privilege of direct access to scholars or religious leaders.

But there's an underlying danger to this convenience. AI is not inherently equipped to deal with the deep, nuanced, and context-heavy nature of religious texts. AI models rely heavily on the data they are trained on, which may not always accurately represent the full depth of religious teachings or may misinterpret sacred meaning when dealing with profound spiritual concepts. This gap can lead to distorted interpretations or even the propagation of harmful misrepresentations of religious beliefs.

The Benefits of AI in Content Creation

Despite the risks, the role of AI in content creation offers undeniable benefits, particularly in making religious knowledge more accessible:

- **Scalability and Reach**: AI enables religious texts and teachings to reach a global audience quickly and efficiently. It breaks down geographical barriers and allows for a wider distribution of religious materials in multiple languages.

- **Cost-Effectiveness**: Producing high-quality religious content traditionally requires the work of scholars, translators, and other experts, often at a significant cost. AI can reduce these costs by automating many of the tasks involved in content creation, such as generating text or translating material.

- **Personalized Learning**: AI systems can be programmed to create personalized religious content for individual users. By analyzing their preferences and learning history, AI can suggest relevant teachings, articles, or sermons that are most likely to resonate with each user.

The Challenges and Pitfalls of AI in Religious Content Creation

While the advantages of AI are clear, the potential pitfalls should not be ignored, particularly in the context of sacred religious knowledge:

- **Lack of Contextual Understanding**: Religious texts are often deeply nuanced and context-dependent. AI, even with the best algorithms, struggles to fully comprehend the cultural, historical, and linguistic context in which sacred texts were revealed. This lack of understanding can result in AI-generated content that is either overly simplistic or outright incorrect.
- **The Risk of Misrepresentation**: Given the importance of accuracy and authenticity in religious knowledge, even minor errors in AI-generated religious content can have far-reaching consequences. A misquoted verse, a misinterpreted hadith, or a distorted concept can potentially change the meaning of an entire religious teaching, leading to confusion and division among followers.
- **Ethical Concerns**: Who is responsible when AI generates misleading or harmful religious content? The ethical responsibility lies with both the developers who create the AI systems and the users who implement them. While AI can be a tool for good, it must be used responsibly, especially in a domain as sensitive as religion.

The Balance Between Technology and Tradition

It's essential to strike a balance between the power of AI and the preservation of sacred knowledge. Religious knowledge is not just a set of facts; it is a living, breathing tradition that has been passed down through generations. The preservation of this tradition requires careful stewardship and a deep understanding of the theological, historical, and cultural contexts that shape it.

AI, as powerful as it is, cannot replace the wisdom and experience of human scholars who are grounded in centuries of tradition and understanding. While AI can help in disseminating religious knowledge more broadly, it should not be relied upon as the sole source of guidance. Human expertise is still essential in interpreting and applying religious teachings in ways that honor their depth and relevance.

Conclusion

In the context of content creation, AI represents a double-edged sword. On one hand, it has the potential to democratize access to religious knowledge, making it more accessible to a global audience. On the other hand, its limitations, particularly in understanding and conveying religious texts accurately, present serious risks. As we continue to integrate AI into religious contexts, it is vital to remain vigilant and discerning, ensuring that we do not sacrifice the authenticity of our sacred knowledge in the pursuit of convenience.

Key Takeaways:

- AI is revolutionizing content creation across various fields, including religious knowledge, making it more accessible to a global audience.
- While AI has significant benefits in terms of scalability, cost-effectiveness, and personalization, it poses risks in religious contexts due to its inability to fully grasp the nuances of sacred texts.
- The challenges of misrepresentation, ethical responsibility, and lack of contextual understanding require careful consideration when using AI to generate religious content.
- A balanced approach that incorporates both AI and human expertise is necessary to ensure the authenticity and integrity of religious knowledge

2.3 The Strengths and Weaknesses of AI

Artificial Intelligence (AI) has the potential to revolutionize many industries by providing innovative solutions and automation at a scale that humans alone cannot achieve. However, as with any technology, its strengths come with accompanying weaknesses. In this section, we will explore the advantages and limitations of AI, especially as it pertains to its role in creating and disseminating content, particularly religious knowledge.

The Strengths of AI

AI's capabilities are continually expanding, allowing it to perform tasks faster, more efficiently, and more accurately than humans in certain areas. Understanding the strengths of AI is crucial for recognizing where it can be an asset, especially in the field of religious content creation.

- **Speed and Efficiency**: One of the most notable strengths of AI is its ability to process vast amounts of data in a fraction of the time it would take a human. This is particularly beneficial when dealing with large databases of religious texts, historical records, or multimedia content. AI can rapidly analyze and cross-reference material, providing insights, summaries, or translations in mere seconds.

- **Consistency and Objectivity**: AI does not suffer from fatigue or emotional bias, which means it can maintain consistent performance throughout its tasks. In religious contexts, AI can provide standardized translations or interpretations of religious texts without the variability that might occur due to human subjectivity. This consistency can help ensure that interpretations are uniform, though this also comes with the risk of oversimplification.

- **Availability and Accessibility**: Unlike human experts who have limited time and availability, AI systems are available 24/7. This allows users from all over the world to access AI-generated content, translations, or recommendations at any time, increasing the global reach of religious knowledge. AI-powered tools can provide on-demand resources such as sermons, prayers, or verses, improving access for people in remote areas or those with limited access to religious scholars.
- **Scalability**: AI can handle an enormous scale of data without the limitations that human capacity might impose. It can process millions of words, analyze complex religious arguments, and even predict patterns across vast collections of texts. This scalability is particularly advantageous in the context of religious education, where the vastness of sacred texts can overwhelm traditional methods of analysis and teaching.
- **Language Translation and Interpretation**: AI has significantly improved in its ability to understand and translate languages. This is especially important in religious contexts where sacred texts are often in languages like Arabic, Hebrew, or Sanskrit. AI-powered translation systems like Google Translate or specialized tools for religious texts can break down language barriers, enabling individuals to access and understand religious teachings in their native languages.

The Weaknesses of AI

Despite its advantages, AI is not without its flaws, particularly when it comes to nuanced, context-dependent areas such as religion. While AI excels in many areas, its limitations must be acknowledged, especially in preserving the depth and authenticity of sacred knowledge.

- **Lack of Contextual Understanding**: AI's most significant weakness lies in its inability to understand the broader context.

While it can identify patterns and make predictions based on data, it does not truly "understand" the meanings behind the information it processes. In religious texts, context is paramount — nuances, historical context, and spiritual significance often shape interpretations. AI lacks the ability to interpret these subtleties, which can lead to misinterpretation or oversimplification.

- **Inability to Grasp Deep Human Emotions**: Religion is deeply tied to human experience, emotions, and spirituality. AI may process religious content, but it cannot experience the emotions, personal struggles, or spiritual journeys that humans undergo when engaging with sacred teachings. This emotional disconnect is particularly problematic when AI is tasked with generating content that is meant to inspire, comfort, or uplift individuals.
- **Risk of Misinformation**: One of the most significant challenges of AI is its potential to propagate misinformation. Because AI systems are trained on existing data, they can easily amplify errors, misunderstandings, or biases present in the source material. In the case of religious texts, AI might generate content that is inaccurate or misleading, particularly if it is drawing from a flawed or incomplete dataset. Since AI lacks the ability to critically evaluate the authenticity of sources, it can unknowingly perpetuate false or distorted teachings.
- **Over-Simplification of Complex Concepts**: Religious knowledge often involves complex theological and philosophical debates that require deep intellectual engagement. AI, however, excels at efficiency and generalization, which means that it may oversimplify intricate religious concepts in a way that detracts from their depth and richness. In doing so, AI risks reducing profound teachings to mere bullet points or slogans, which can dilute their transformative power.

- **Dependence on Data Quality**: AI is only as good as the data it is trained on. If the data used to train the system is incomplete, biased, or inaccurate, the output will reflect those shortcomings. In religious content, where precision and authenticity are paramount, poor-quality data can lead to significant errors. Additionally, if AI is trained on content that is not representative of a diverse range of religious perspectives, it may inadvertently favor one interpretation over others, leading to an imbalanced view of religious teachings.
- **Ethical Concerns**: The use of AI in religious contexts also raises ethical concerns about the role of technology in shaping human beliefs and practices. While AI can enhance accessibility to religious knowledge, there is a risk that it could replace the role of human scholars, leading to the commodification of sacred texts. Moreover, the use of AI to create religious content without the involvement of human experts raises questions about the authenticity and legitimacy of such content. Is it appropriate for machines to play a significant role in shaping spiritual understanding?

Striking the Balance: Harnessing AI's Strengths While Addressing Its Weaknesses

While the strengths of AI make it an invaluable tool in many fields, including religious knowledge dissemination, its weaknesses must be taken into account when integrating AI into the creation and distribution of sacred content. A balanced approach is essential to ensure that AI is used responsibly, with careful consideration given to the limitations of technology.

Leveraging AI's Strengths:

- AI can be harnessed to automate certain tasks, such as translating religious texts, generating content for educational purposes, or creating accessible summaries. These tasks can save time and make religious knowledge more widely accessible.

Addressing AI's Weaknesses:

- However, it is crucial that AI-generated content be carefully vetted and verified by human experts. Religious scholars, who possess deep contextual understanding, must play an active role in ensuring that AI-generated material is accurate, authentic, and sensitive to the nuances of religious teachings.

Conclusion: Recognizing AI's Role with Caution and Responsibility

AI is a powerful tool with immense potential in a wide range of applications, including the dissemination of religious knowledge. However, its limitations cannot be ignored. While AI offers speed, consistency, and scalability, it is still far from perfect. It cannot understand the depth and complexity of human emotions or the nuances inherent in sacred texts. As such, AI should be seen as an assistant, not a replacement, in the field of religious scholarship.

By recognizing both the strengths and weaknesses of AI, we can ensure that its application in religious contexts is both responsible and respectful of the sacredness of religious knowledge. In doing so, we can harness the power of AI to enhance religious education and engagement, without compromising the authenticity or depth of the content it generates.

2.4 When Algorithms Preach: Hidden Dangers of AI Theology

As Artificial Intelligence (AI) continues to evolve and infiltrate every aspect of society, its use in religious contexts raises unique concerns that are not immediately apparent. While AI can offer great benefits in terms of accessibility and efficiency, it also presents risks that can significantly impact the authenticity and integrity of religious knowledge. In this section, we will explore the unseen risks of using AI in religious settings, considering the consequences of misinterpretation, over-reliance, and the erosion of traditional religious scholarship.

The Erosion of Traditional Religious Scholarship

AI's involvement in religious content creation and dissemination risks undermining centuries of tradition in religious scholarship. Scholars, who have spent decades studying religious texts and interpreting them within the appropriate historical, cultural, and spiritual contexts, play an irreplaceable role in preserving the integrity of religious knowledge.

- **The Authority of Human Scholars**: Traditional religious scholars possess not only knowledge but also wisdom gained through years of study, experience, and spiritual growth. They have a unique ability to discern the deeper meanings behind texts, taking into account historical context, cultural nuances, and theological significance. AI, by contrast, lacks the human experience and intuition necessary to grasp the full depth of sacred teachings.
- **The Risk of Dehumanization**: AI-generated religious content, devoid of human insight, may lead to a form of "dehumanization" of faith, where personal spiritual journeys and the wisdom of religious leaders are replaced by algorithms. This threatens to reduce religion to a mere transactional experience, devoid of the human connection that is essential to the practice of faith.

- **The Loss of Spiritual Authority**: Religious scholars, imams, and clergy have long served as spiritual guides, offering interpretations, guidance, and advice based on years of training. AI's ability to generate content might diminish the perceived authority of human religious leaders, making individuals more reliant on machine-generated interpretations. This could dilute the personal connection between believers and their spiritual mentors, weakening the overall quality of religious guidance.

The Risk of Misinterpretation and Oversimplification

Religious texts are inherently complex and open to multiple interpretations. In the hands of AI, these texts may be misinterpreted or oversimplified, leading to content that is inaccurate or misleading.

- **Contextual Misinterpretation**: One of the greatest risks of AI in religious contexts is its inability to understand the depth of context. AI works by recognizing patterns in data, but it does not truly comprehend the nuances of human experience, emotion, or history. This makes it prone to misinterpreting sacred texts, especially when dealing with metaphorical, allegorical, or culturally specific language.
- **Simplification of Complex Doctrines**: Religion often deals with complex theological concepts and intricate philosophical debates. AI's tendency to reduce information to its simplest form for easy consumption may lead to oversimplification. What is lost in this process is the complexity and depth of religious teachings, which are vital for a well-rounded understanding of faith. Such simplification could undermine the richness of religious knowledge, leaving believers with a shallow, incomplete view of their faith.
- **Potential for Distorted Doctrines**: AI systems generate content based on patterns learned from existing data. If the data fed into these systems contains errors, biases, or distortions, the AI will

replicate and propagate those inaccuracies. In the context of religion, even a small misinterpretation can have profound effects, potentially leading to doctrinal shifts or the spread of incorrect teachings. AI lacks the discernment to identify the subtle theological distinctions that often separate accurate interpretations from erroneous ones.

The Creation of Echo Chambers

Another significant risk of using AI in religious contexts is the potential for AI to create echo chambers — environments in which users are exposed only to content that reinforces their existing beliefs and biases.

- **Algorithmic Bias**: AI systems are designed to provide content based on user preferences and behavior, often reinforcing what users already believe. In religious settings, this could lead to the creation of echo chambers where individuals are only exposed to interpretations and teachings that align with their preexisting views. This can result in the narrowing of religious perspectives, making it more difficult for believers to engage with diverse viewpoints or alternative interpretations.
- **Polarization**: In religious contexts, echo chambers can contribute to the fragmentation of communities. AI systems that prioritize content based on user preferences can exacerbate existing divisions, reinforcing extremist views and creating polarization within religious communities. This can hinder constructive dialogue, reduce empathy, and deepen sectarian divides, ultimately undermining the unity and common values that should bind believers together.
- **Reduced Exposure to Counterarguments**: Echo chambers created by AI can also limit exposure to counterarguments or alternative interpretations, which are essential for the growth of knowledge and understanding. In religious education, exposure to

diverse perspectives is vital for developing a well-rounded understanding of faith. When AI systems prioritize content that aligns with a user's existing beliefs, they may prevent individuals from critically engaging with opposing views, potentially leading to intellectual stagnation.

Over-Reliance on AI for Spiritual Guidance

AI has the potential to provide quick, automated answers to religious questions. However, over-reliance on AI for spiritual guidance carries several risks, as it can replace the need for human connection, personalized advice, and critical reflection.

- **Lack of Personalization**: AI, no matter how sophisticated, cannot offer personalized spiritual advice in the same way a human scholar or mentor can. Spirituality is deeply personal and often requires empathy, understanding, and tailored guidance based on an individual's unique circumstances. AI-generated responses, however, are generic and cannot account for the complexities of a person's spiritual journey or life situation. Over-reliance on AI for such guidance risks undermining the importance of human interaction in the practice of faith.
- **Decreased Spiritual Reflection**: AI can provide answers quickly and efficiently, but it does not encourage deep reflection or contemplation. In religion, reflection is often central to the process of learning, growing, and connecting with one's faith. By relying too heavily on AI, individuals may miss out on the opportunities for introspection and spiritual development that come from engaging with religious texts and seeking guidance from human mentors.
- **The Danger of Mechanical Spirituality**: Over-relying on AI in religious matters may also lead to the reduction of spirituality to mechanical processes. If people begin to treat religious practices and beliefs as mere algorithms to be followed, it could lead to a

more transactional approach to faith, devoid of the personal connection and emotional depth that makes spirituality meaningful.

The Risk of Alienation from Traditional Communities

Religious communities have long been spaces for fellowship, mutual support, and spiritual growth. As AI becomes more integrated into the religious landscape, there is a risk that people may become alienated from their traditional religious communities.

- **Isolation and Disconnection**: The more people turn to AI for religious knowledge and guidance, the less they may engage with their local religious communities. In many faiths, the communal aspect of worship, study, and reflection is essential to the spiritual experience. AI cannot replicate the social and emotional aspects of belonging to a religious community, and relying on AI could lead to spiritual isolation and a weakened sense of community.
- **Undermining the Role of Religious Leaders**: As AI-generated content becomes more common, there is a risk that the role of human religious leaders and mentors could be undermined. AI-generated sermons, prayers, and teachings might replace the need for human interaction, diminishing the role of clergy and lay leaders who have traditionally guided their communities in matters of faith and practice.
- **Loss of Intergenerational Knowledge**: Religious communities have long passed down knowledge through generations, with older generations imparting wisdom to the younger. AI cannot replace this intergenerational transfer of knowledge, which is vital for preserving religious traditions and cultural heritage. As AI grows in prominence, there is a risk that this essential knowledge transfer could be disrupted.

Conclusion: A Call for Caution and Responsibility

AI presents both tremendous opportunities and significant risks, particularly when it comes to the realm of religion. While it can enhance access to religious knowledge and streamline content creation, the unseen risks — such as the erosion of traditional scholarship, misinterpretation, and the creation of echo chambers — must be carefully considered. It is essential that AI is integrated into religious contexts with caution and responsibility, ensuring that the authenticity and richness of sacred knowledge are preserved.

Religious communities and scholars must be proactive in addressing these risks, using AI as a tool to complement, rather than replace, human interaction, insight, and wisdom. As AI continues to evolve, it is crucial to maintain a balance between technological advancement and the timeless values of faith, human connection, and spiritual growth.

Chapter 3: The Causes of AI Error

3.1 The Nature of AI's Mistakes

As AI becomes more involved in generating religious content, one of the most concerning issues is the potential for misquoting sacred texts. While AI systems are designed to learn and process vast amounts of data, they are not immune to errors — especially when it comes to the complexity and nuance inherent in religious scriptures. In this section, we will explore how AI's limitations in understanding context, interpreting language, and handling sacred texts can lead to mistakes that significantly affect the accuracy of religious quotes.

The Complexity of Religious Texts

Religious texts such as the Quran, the Bible, and the Hadith collections are rich with layers of meaning, historical context, and interpretive depth. Unlike simple factual statements, these texts are often written in complex, metaphorical, and allegorical language. To accurately understand and convey the message of these texts requires a deep understanding of theology, history, language, and culture — all of which pose significant challenges for AI systems.

- **Contextual Nuance**: Religious texts are highly contextual. Verses and statements may have different meanings depending on the situation in which they were revealed or the circumstances under which they are being interpreted. For example, a verse in the Quran that addresses a specific event in history may be misinterpreted when read out of context. AI, which relies on pattern recognition and data input, cannot always grasp these subtleties, making it prone to misquoting or misinterpreting these texts.
- **The Role of Interpretation (Tafsir and Exegesis)**: Religious scholars spend years studying the nuances of sacred texts through the lens of tafsir (Quranic exegesis) and other methods of interpretation. They consider not only the words themselves but also the context, grammar, and historical setting in which the text

was revealed. AI, however, does not possess this interpretive capacity and is not capable of engaging in nuanced exegesis. This lack of interpretive depth can lead to errors in quoting religious texts.

- **Metaphor and Symbolism**: Many religious texts are filled with metaphors, parables, and symbolic language. AI systems, which process information through algorithms and pattern recognition, are not equipped to fully understand these literary devices. The inability to grasp symbolic language can lead to AI misrepresenting or distorting the true meaning of a religious text. For example, a verse that uses metaphorical language about light and darkness might be misquoted as a literal description, thus changing its intended message.

The Limitations of Machine Learning

AI systems, particularly those that rely on machine learning, can only function within the boundaries of the data they are trained on. When it comes to sacred texts, the scope of this data is crucial to ensuring accuracy. However, the complexity of language, translation variations, and the absence of complete datasets pose significant challenges.

- **Data-Driven Errors**: AI systems operate by recognizing patterns in large datasets. However, these datasets may contain errors or inconsistencies, which AI can unknowingly perpetuate. For example, a dataset that includes multiple translations of a religious text might feature variations in wording that are due to differences in translator interpretations. When AI processes these variations, it may generate an incorrect or misleading quote based on an unreliable or inconsistent dataset.
- **Translation Challenges**: Sacred texts like the Quran and the Bible have been translated into many languages. Each translation comes with its own set of linguistic and cultural challenges. Machine learning models, trained on various translations, may not

always capture the depth or accuracy of the original text. Even slight errors in translation can lead to significant misquotations. For example, a verse translated as "peace" in English may originally have a much richer meaning, such as "submission to God," which AI may overlook if it is not well-versed in the nuances of Arabic or ancient languages.

- **Inadequate Training on Religious Texts**: AI systems designed for general content creation are often trained on a broad range of materials, including news articles, blogs, and other online content. However, they may not have been specifically trained to handle religious texts with the care and expertise they require. Without specialized training in religious language, theology, and interpretation, AI is more likely to make errors in quoting religious texts. The absence of specialized datasets focused on religious texts further exacerbates this issue.

Lack of Human Insight and Intuition

AI lacks human insight, intuition, and the ability to consider the spiritual, emotional, and cultural significance of religious texts. These texts are not simply a collection of words; they are considered sacred and are believed to carry deep spiritual meaning. Understanding the impact and weight of these texts requires more than just an intellectual grasp — it requires spiritual insight, empathy, and experience.

- **The Absence of Spiritual Understanding**: AI does not possess spiritual consciousness or an understanding of faith. Religious texts are not just intellectual exercises; they are deeply intertwined with the lived experiences of believers. AI, however, processes texts as information without understanding the spiritual dimensions. A verse that might resonate deeply with a person of faith may not be understood in the same way by a machine.
- **Emotional and Psychological Impact**: Religious texts are often written to provoke deep emotional and psychological responses. A

quote from a sacred text may serve as a source of comfort, strength, or hope for believers. AI, by contrast, lacks the ability to understand these emotional dimensions. It cannot assess how a misquote might affect the reader, emotionally or spiritually. This lack of sensitivity can lead to AI-generated quotes that are technically accurate but spiritually hollow, failing to convey the text's intended message.

- **The Role of the Human Heart**: Religious teachings emphasize the importance of the heart — not just the intellect — in understanding and living according to divine guidance. Human scholars, who interpret sacred texts, do so with both the mind and the heart, considering not only the words but also the spiritual message. AI, however, lacks this dual capacity and is therefore limited in its ability to capture the holistic nature of religious texts.

The Risk of Misleading Content

One of the most concerning aspects of AI-generated religious content is the risk of producing misleading or completely incorrect quotes. Given the AI's lack of true understanding of religious texts, there is a significant risk that the content it generates may be misleading, leading individuals to form incorrect theological conclusions.

- **AI's Inability to Discern Intent**: The intention behind a religious text is as important as the words themselves. Human scholars are able to understand the intent of a passage — whether it is meant to be a commandment, a story, a metaphor, or a moral lesson. AI lacks this ability to discern intent. Without understanding the purpose behind the words, AI may quote them in ways that distort or misrepresent the original message, leading to confusion or the spread of erroneous beliefs.
- **Consequences of Misleading Quotes**: In the digital age, information spreads quickly and widely. A misquoted religious text, especially one that appears to come from an authoritative

source, can gain traction online, spreading misinformation to thousands, if not millions, of people. This can lead to the distortion of religious understanding on a global scale. The rapid dissemination of misleading content creates long-term theological and spiritual confusion that is difficult to correct.

- **The Danger of "Fake Knowledge"**: The proliferation of AI-generated quotes that are inaccurate or incomplete contributes to the spread of "fake knowledge." People may unknowingly share or base their beliefs on these inaccurate quotes, perpetuating misconceptions and undermining the integrity of religious teachings. In some cases, this misinformation may even be used to justify harmful practices or beliefs that contradict the core principles of faith.

Conclusion: A Call for Vigilance

The nature of AI's mistakes in quoting religious texts is a serious concern that must not be ignored. While AI can offer valuable tools for learning and content generation, its inability to fully comprehend the complexity, context, and spiritual significance of sacred texts can lead to significant errors. The risks of misinterpretation, misleading content, and the erosion of traditional religious scholarship make it essential for believers to approach AI-generated religious content with caution and critical awareness. As we continue to integrate AI into religious contexts, it is crucial that we safeguard the integrity of sacred knowledge, ensuring that human scholars and religious leaders remain the primary sources of religious guidance. Only by maintaining a balance between technological advancements and traditional scholarship can we ensure that religious knowledge remains pure and untainted.

3.2 The Limits of AI in Understanding Context and Nuance

In recent years, artificial intelligence (AI) has demonstrated its immense potential in fields ranging from healthcare to entertainment, and it has even begun to make inroads into domains that involve complex human knowledge systems. However, one of the most challenging areas for AI remains the interpretation and understanding of religious texts, which require a deep grasp of cultural, linguistic, historical, and spiritual contexts. While AI has made strides in processing vast amounts of data and generating content, it is still fundamentally limited in its ability to understand and interpret the nuances embedded within sacred writings such as the Quran, Hadith, and other religious scriptures. This section will explore these limitations, examining how AI struggles to appreciate the contextual and nuanced aspects of religious knowledge.

Linguistic Challenges: AI's Struggle with Language and Semantics

One of the most fundamental challenges that AI faces in interpreting religious texts is its inability to fully understand the subtleties of language. The Quran, Hadith, and many other sacred texts are written in highly sophisticated, layered, and often poetic language that includes idioms, metaphors, and historical references. The nuances of meaning embedded within these texts are often beyond the reach of algorithms that are designed to process language in a literal and analytical manner.

Take, for example, the Arabic language in which the Quran was revealed. Arabic is a rich and complex language, and one word can carry multiple meanings depending on the context in which it is used. Many Quranic verses, for instance, require an understanding of historical circumstances, cultural implications, and theological concepts in order to grasp their true meaning. AI, however, operates on pattern recognition and statistical models, which means it may fail to discern the various layers of meaning embedded in words and phrases.

Moreover, AI lacks an understanding of syntax, grammar, and the underlying social and religious norms that shape language use in sacred contexts. A word that appears in one context may hold vastly different implications when it is used in another. For example, the Arabic word "hijab" can mean "veil" or "covering," but its significance extends far beyond mere physical covering—it is tied to a deeper spiritual and social concept in Islam. AI might process the word accurately in a literal sense, but it could miss its deeper connotations regarding modesty, identity, and societal values. In this way, AI's mechanical approach to language poses a major challenge in accurately interpreting the text of the Quran or Hadith.

The Role of Context in Religious Texts

AI also struggles to understand the context surrounding religious texts. The Quran and Hadith are not standalone statements; they are embedded within a broader historical, social, and theological framework. The Quranic verses, for example, were revealed in specific historical situations, with reasons for revelation (Asbab al-Nuzul) that are critical for understanding their meaning. AI is not capable of accessing the contextual background that surrounds a verse, nor can it account for the lived realities of the early Muslim community, the Prophet's (PBUH) companions, or the socio-political events that shaped the interpretation of these verses.

Many religious scholars emphasize the importance of understanding the historical context when interpreting religious texts. Without a firm grasp of Asbab al-Nuzul, AI would fail to provide an accurate or complete interpretation of certain verses. This is particularly problematic in the case of verses that were revealed in response to specific events or questions. Without understanding the context of these revelations, an AI could easily misinterpret the meaning, leading to misleading or even harmful conclusions. For instance, the famous verse "There is no compulsion in religion" (Quran 2:256) can easily be misunderstood without an understanding of the specific situation in which it was revealed—a situation where some people were being forced to accept Islam against their will. AI may fail to grasp this historical nuance and apply the verse to a broader, out-of-context scenario.

Furthermore, in religious interpretations, the context often includes the interaction between the Prophet (PBUH) and his companions. The Prophet's sayings and actions (Hadith) are deeply rooted in the social norms and practices of his time, as well as in the spiritual concerns of the early Muslim community. AI cannot replicate the ability of scholars who engage in the painstaking work of comparing Hadith, understanding their context, and applying them to new situations. Without this contextual awareness, AI-generated interpretations may be shallow or incomplete.

The Complexities of Interpretation: Tafsir and Scholarly Debate

Religious texts, especially the Quran, are not always straightforward in their meaning. The Quran often contains verses that are clear in meaning (muhkamat) as well as verses whose meanings are ambiguous or open to interpretation (mutashabihat). Understanding these verses requires the nuanced approach of tafsir (exegesis), a field of study developed over centuries by Islamic scholars. Tafsir is not simply an exercise in translating words—it involves a deep understanding of the historical, linguistic, and theological dimensions of the text. Scholars engage with the text from multiple perspectives, drawing on a wide range of sources, including Hadith, the opinions of earlier scholars, and consensus (ijma) from the Muslim community.

AI, on the other hand, lacks the intellectual depth and the theological training necessary for such an endeavor. While AI can analyze patterns and correlations in the text, it cannot engage in the kind of sophisticated scholarly interpretation that has been developed over centuries. For example, the process of deriving legal rulings (fiqh) from the Quran requires careful reasoning (ijtihad) and the application of principles that have been refined by scholars over generations. AI cannot replicate this process of reasoning or account for the ethical and legal implications of a particular interpretation. It might provide a mechanical or overly simplistic interpretation of a verse, but it cannot weigh the moral, legal, and spiritual complexities that scholars consider.

The challenge of AI's lack of scholarly engagement is particularly significant when it comes to ambiguous verses or controversial issues in Islamic jurisprudence. In these cases, scholars rely on their training, intellectual rigor, and experience to provide a nuanced interpretation. AI, by contrast, lacks this ability to engage in the intellectual debate that is crucial to Islamic scholarship. Thus, while AI may be able to generate a generic interpretation of a verse, it cannot provide the depth of analysis and critical engagement that scholars offer.

AI's Inability to Grasp the Spiritual and Emotional Dimensions of Religious Texts

Another important limitation of AI is its inability to grasp the spiritual and emotional dimensions of religious texts. Religious texts are not merely intellectual exercises—they are meant to inspire faith, guide moral behavior, and provide solace and comfort to believers. AI, however, lacks the emotional and spiritual intelligence required to understand the deeper, transformative role that religious teachings play in the lives of individuals and communities.

For example, the Quran is not just a book of laws and regulations; it is a source of spiritual guidance, meant to connect the believer with the Divine. The Quranic verses are recited with an understanding of their spiritual weight, and many verses are meant to evoke emotions such as hope, fear, gratitude, and awe. AI lacks the capacity to experience or understand these emotions, and thus, it cannot fully convey the affective power of the Quranic text. A verse about God's mercy, for instance, is not merely a statement of fact—it is meant to inspire the believer to feel a deep connection to God's love and compassion. AI can process the words, but it cannot replicate the emotional and spiritual experience that those words are meant to evoke.

This emotional and spiritual resonance is something that is deeply human, and it is something that AI can never truly replicate. While AI can be useful as a tool for generating content and answering basic questions, it cannot replace the deep, transformative experience that believers undergo when they engage with the Quran, Hadith, or other sacred texts.

Conclusion: The Need for Human Oversight

While AI can aid research and content generation in religious contexts, it cannot replace scholars in interpreting sacred texts, which require deep linguistic, historical, and spiritual understanding. Despite technological advances, AI lacks the human insight essential for authentic interpretation. Therefore, AI-generated religious content must always be reviewed by qualified scholars. Ultimately, technology remains a helpful tool, but the responsibility to preserve and transmit religious wisdom rests with human beings guided by faith and tradition.

3.3 Why AI Can't Be Trusted with Sacred Knowledge

As artificial intelligence continues to evolve, it offers vast potential in many sectors, including content generation, language translation, and information retrieval. However, one area where AI is not equipped to handle with precision and responsibility is the transmission of sacred knowledge. Religious texts, be they from the Quran, the Bible, the Torah, or any other scripture, contain profound layers of meaning, historical context, and spiritual depth. AI, despite its advancements, simply cannot fully comprehend or preserve these aspects. This section explores the key reasons why AI cannot be trusted to accurately quote or interpret sacred knowledge.

The Limitations of AI's Understanding of Context

Religious texts are not just a collection of words; they are filled with context, subtleties, and layers of meaning. The Quran, for example, contains verses that were revealed in specific historical contexts, addressing particular circumstances, events, and people. The Bible includes parables, metaphors, and idiomatic expressions that require cultural and theological understanding to interpret correctly. AI, on the other hand, processes text based on algorithms and statistical patterns, not understanding.

- **Lack of Spiritual Insight**

  AI systems operate by recognizing patterns in data. They excel in analyzing large datasets and predicting outcomes based on statistical trends. However, spiritual insight is not something that can be reduced to patterns. A verse from the Quran or the Bible, for instance, may not only have a historical context but also multiple layers of spiritual interpretation, depending on one's faith, intention, or situation. AI lacks the intrinsic ability to grasp the deeper meanings and subtleties that a human theologian or religious scholar would. Its understanding is purely mechanical and superficial.

- **Ignoring Historical Context**

  AI is often trained on texts without a full understanding of the historical or social context in which these texts were revealed or written. A verse of scripture, when placed in its proper context, may offer a completely different interpretation than when viewed in isolation. The Quran, for instance, contains verses that were revealed to respond to specific situations during the life of Prophet Muhammad (PBUH). Without understanding the socio-political circumstances, AI might misinterpret the meaning of a verse, leading to an inaccurate or skewed understanding.

AI Lacks a True Understanding of Intent and Nuance

Religious texts are not just a set of instructions or laws; they are also expressions of divine wisdom, and often, they communicate complex moral and ethical principles. Humans interpret these principles based on their spiritual maturity, understanding, and intent. AI lacks the ability to understand the nuanced intent behind religious teachings or the moral and ethical weight they carry.

- **Absence of Moral Judgment**

  In religious discussions, the intent of the speaker or writer is as important as the words themselves. In the Quran, for example, there are many verses that encourage believers to act with mercy, kindness, and justice. AI, however, cannot understand the nuances of mercy or kindness—concepts that require emotional intelligence and moral judgment. AI models are devoid of empathy, compassion, and the deep moral reflection required to interpret such concepts meaningfully.

- **Inability to Recognize Theological Implications**

  Theological discussions often delve into questions of purpose, existence, and divine will. These discussions require a deep understanding of the nature of God, the role of humans, and the interconnectedness of creation. AI, which works based on algorithms and logic, cannot comprehend these theological implications. For example, in interpreting verses that relate to the nature of God, AI cannot grasp the divine attributes as understood by various religious traditions. It lacks the spiritual and philosophical depth necessary for such discussions.

AI's Reliance on Data Rather Than Wisdom

AI is built to process data, but wisdom is not merely the accumulation of data. Wisdom involves the ability to apply knowledge in ways that reflect understanding, compassion, and judgment. Religious knowledge is not just an informational resource to be processed; it is a living tradition that requires a deep, evolving understanding of human experience and the divine.

- **Data-Driven but Spiritually Shallow**

  AI's power lies in its ability to work with vast amounts of data and recognize patterns within that data. However, religious knowledge is not merely a matter of compiling data. It is about understanding the soul of the text, the divine message, and its application in the life of the believer. AI's data-driven approach fails to capture the spiritual essence of religious knowledge. For example, in interpreting religious rituals or prayers, AI cannot fathom the inner experience of devotion, reverence, or submission that a believer might feel. Thus, while AI may correctly quote a verse or prayer, it cannot replicate the spiritual depth with which it is recited or understood.

- **Misleading Oversimplification**

  AI, in its attempt to simplify complex issues for users, may present religious knowledge in an oversimplified form. This is especially true when AI generates summaries or quick answers to religious queries. In its bid to be helpful, AI might strip away the complexities, contradictions, and richness that exist within religious discourse. For instance, Islamic law (Sharia) is a complex system based on the Quran, Hadith, and scholarly consensus. AI, without understanding the full depth of these sources, may present an oversimplified version that misleads the user into believing that the law is rigid and unchanging when, in reality, it is flexible and nuanced.

The Risk of Perpetuating Misinformation

Even if AI produces quotes or interpretations based on accurate data, the lack of verification in its processes can lead to the spread of misinformation. Sacred texts are frequently misquoted due to AI's inability to filter out incorrect interpretations or sources. The AI's reliance on open-source data from potentially unreliable platforms can lead to the amplification of incorrect information, which may then be perpetuated across the digital space.

- **The Chain Reaction of Misinformation**

  Once AI generates and spreads a misquote, it is easy for this information to become viral, especially in today's interconnected world. Social media platforms, websites, and other digital channels make it easy for content to be shared, reshared, and disseminated. A single misquote of a sacred verse can thus spread quickly, and correcting this error becomes increasingly difficult as the misinformation multiplies.

- **The Need for Human Oversight**

  To prevent the spread of misinformation, AI-generated content, especially when dealing with sacred texts, must be carefully supervised by human experts. Religious scholars, theologians, and those with deep knowledge of sacred traditions must be involved in the content verification process. Without this oversight, AI can contribute to the distortion of religious truths and practices, leading to confusion and division among believers.

Conclusion: The Need for Caution and Human Expertise

While artificial intelligence can be a valuable tool for a variety of purposes, sacred knowledge is not one of them. AI's limitations in understanding context, intent, and nuance make it ill-suited for handling the profound teachings found in religious texts. The importance of human expertise—especially the involvement of religious scholars and theologians—cannot be overstated. As AI continues to evolve, it is essential that we remain vigilant and mindful of its role in religious education and discourse. Sacred texts demand respect, careful interpretation, and wisdom—qualities that AI, for all its strengths, cannot provide.

3.4 The Danger of Blind Trust in Technology

In an era where technology permeates every aspect of life, there is a growing tendency to place blind trust in machines and algorithms. This phenomenon is particularly dangerous when it involves religious knowledge, which is sacred and deeply nuanced. While AI offers incredible benefits, including accessibility and speed, it also carries significant risks—especially when used as the sole authority in interpreting or quoting religious texts. This section highlights the inherent dangers of trusting technology without scrutiny, particularly in the context of sacred knowledge.

Technology Cannot Replace Human Judgment

AI systems, at their core, are designed to make decisions based on data. They can process massive amounts of information quickly and often arrive at conclusions that seem logical based on the available data. However, this approach leaves out one critical component that is irreplaceable: human judgment. When it comes to religious texts, human judgment is essential for interpreting meaning, understanding context, and applying wisdom.

- **Lack of Emotional and Spiritual Understanding**

  AI does not possess the capability to understand or process emotions. Religious texts are not just informational—they are often deeply emotional and spiritual. The Quran, for example, contains verses that speak to the soul, addressing not only intellectual comprehension but also spiritual transformation. AI lacks the ability to resonate with the heart of the believer. A verse that offers comfort to the grieving, guidance for the lost, or solace for the anxious cannot be fully understood by a machine that only processes information in binary terms.

- **The Role of Wisdom in Interpretation**

  Human judgment is informed by wisdom, experience, and cultural context. AI, however, makes decisions based on patterns in data, often disregarding the deeper implications of its conclusions. In religious contexts, this can result in overly simplistic interpretations that miss the richness and depth of the text. The judgment of a scholar or a religious authority is informed by years of study, reflection, and spiritual insight, which are qualities AI cannot replicate.

The Risk of AI Promoting Narrow or Biased Interpretations

AI operates by identifying patterns in data and applying these patterns to generate conclusions. While this process works well for many tasks, it can result in narrow or biased interpretations when applied to religious texts. AI's data sources are often limited to the information it is fed, which may reflect the biases of the programmers, the data, or the platform from which the data is sourced.

- **Bias in Training Data**

  The data used to train AI is not always objective or neutral. If the data used to train a machine contains biases—whether religious, cultural, or ideological—those biases can be reflected in the AI's output. For instance, an AI trained on a particular interpretation of a religious text may unknowingly propagate that interpretation as the "correct" one, despite other valid interpretations. In the case of religious knowledge, this bias can be particularly damaging, as it can distort the message of the sacred text and potentially lead to sectarian division.

- **Over-Simplification of Complex Doctrines**

  Religious texts often contain complex theological ideas and diverse interpretations. AI may oversimplify these concepts, leading to a reductionist approach to deeply philosophical and spiritual questions. In Islam, for example, issues related to Sharia law, spiritual practice, or the nature of God are not straightforward; they involve centuries of scholarship and nuanced understanding. AI, however, might reduce these rich traditions to short, clipped answers that fail to honor their depth.

The Perils of Relying on AI for Religious Authority

As AI begins to play a larger role in content generation, there is a danger that it may begin to be viewed as an authority in areas where human expertise should remain supreme. This is particularly true in the realm of religion, where guidance is often sought for deeply personal, existential, and moral matters. The danger arises when individuals begin to view AI-generated content as a substitute for expert religious guidance or as a source of absolute truth.

- **Undermining the Role of Scholars and Religious Leaders**

  Religious scholars and leaders have a vital role in guiding the community. They interpret sacred texts with authority and have the responsibility to ensure that their interpretations align with centuries of established scholarship. By relying too heavily on AI for religious information, there is a risk of undermining the essential role that human experts play in maintaining the integrity of religious practice. AI does not have the capacity to engage in the rigorous scholarship required to interpret religious texts properly, and relying on it for spiritual guidance can lead to misguided or incorrect beliefs.

- **Overreliance on Convenience**

  One of the greatest risks of blind trust in technology is the growing convenience that comes with it. People increasingly rely on technology because it is quick, easy, and often more accessible than traditional forms of knowledge. However, convenience should not come at the cost of wisdom and responsibility. When it comes to religious knowledge, convenience can lead to superficial understanding. Sacred texts require contemplation, deep thought, and reflection, none of which AI can provide. Relying on AI as a quick source of answers for complex spiritual or theological questions can result in a shallow understanding of the material and ultimately undermine the richness of religious practice.

The Importance of Human Responsibility in Handling Sacred Texts

Technology has made access to information more convenient than ever, but this convenience comes with a significant responsibility. The widespread use of AI to disseminate religious knowledge means that individuals must take on greater responsibility in verifying the content they encounter. Blindly trusting AI without questioning its outputs can lead to the spread of misinformation, confusion, and misinterpretation.

- **Critical Thinking and Verification**

  The need for critical thinking has never been more important. Just as individuals should not blindly trust any single source of information, the same applies to AI-generated content. Sacred texts are not just historical documents; they are living sources of guidance that impact the lives of believers. Verification is essential to ensure that what we learn and share aligns with the truth as understood by scholars, religious authorities, and the community. The onus is on individuals to verify information before accepting it as authentic, especially when it pertains to religious texts.

- **Collaboration Between AI and Religious Experts**

  Rather than viewing AI as an adversary or a replacement for human scholarship, it is crucial to explore how AI can be used in collaboration with religious experts. AI can assist scholars by providing large datasets, organizing information, and performing analyses that help in the interpretation of religious texts. However, AI should never replace the role of human scholars who bring the wisdom, insight, and authority necessary to interpret sacred knowledge accurately.

Conclusion: Moving Beyond Blind Trust

While AI has tremendous potential to enhance our lives and provide valuable insights, blind trust in technology—especially in areas as sacred and sensitive as religious knowledge—can be dangerous. AI lacks the depth of understanding, emotional resonance, and moral judgment required to interpret religious texts responsibly. As technology continues to evolve, it is essential that we maintain a balanced approach, using AI as a tool to complement human judgment, not replace it. Blind trust in AI can lead to misinterpretations, misinformation, and the erosion of religious authority. By embracing a thoughtful, collaborative approach to AI, we can preserve the sanctity of sacred knowledge and ensure that it remains a source of true guidance for generations to come.

Chapter 4: The Imperative to Verify for Authenticity

4.1 Verification as a Religious Duty

In an age dominated by technology, the need for verification has never been more urgent. With the rise of digital misinformation, unchecked content, and AI-generated errors, ensuring the authenticity of information is not just an intellectual obligation but a religious one. Islam, like many other faiths, places great emphasis on verifying information before accepting it as truth. This duty is integral not only to maintaining the purity of knowledge but also to protecting individuals, communities, and faith itself from falsehoods.

The Quranic Foundation for Verification

In Islam, the pursuit of truth and accuracy is not merely encouraged but is seen as a moral and religious obligation. Verification is not a passive act—it is a proactive duty that prevents the spread of falsehood and ensures the integrity of the information we encounter. As we live in an age where misinformation can spread faster than ever, the teachings of the Quran serve as a timeless reminder of the importance of verifying the information we receive.

> *"O you who have believed, if there comes to you a disobedient person with information, investigate, lest you harm a people out of ignorance and become, over what you have done, regretful."* (Quran 49:6)

In the context of modern information, the phrase "a disobedient person" can be understood as referring to any source of information that is unreliable or unverified—whether it comes from individuals, media outlets, or digital platforms. Just as the Quran warns against accepting information from a person whose intentions may be questionable, today's equivalent would be any means of communication that may spread falsehoods, rumors, or unverified claims.

This verse highlights the necessity of careful investigation and verification before acting on any information. The consequences of failing to verify can lead to harm, regret, and injustice, making it a serious responsibility for every Muslim to ensure accuracy and prevent the spread of falsehood.

The Sacred Duty to Protect Religious Truth

Every religion, whether Christianity, Judaism, Islam, Hinduism, Buddhism, or others, emphasizes the importance of truth. In the digital age, this sacred duty extends to ensuring the content we engage with, share, and propagate online is accurate and trustworthy. Sacred texts across all traditions stress that truth is a divine principle, and by adhering to this truth, we align ourselves with the will of the Creator.

- **Religious Teachings on Truth:** In Christianity, the Bible emphasizes, "You will know the truth, and the truth will set you free" (John 8:32), indicating the paramount importance of truth in religious life. Similarly, in Hinduism, the pursuit of truth is a fundamental goal, as expressed in the ancient teachings of the Upanishads and the Bhagavad Gita. In Buddhism, the principle of "Right Speech" from the Eightfold Path calls for truthfulness in communication. These universal teachings highlight that truth is not just a moral virtue but a divine mandate.
- **Religious Integrity in the Digital Era:** With the advent of digital platforms, the spreading of misinformation has become more rampant than ever. Therefore, it is the religious responsibility of every individual to ensure that what they share is aligned with the sacred teachings of their faith. Whether one is sharing a verse from the Bible, a quote from the Quran, or a passage from the Torah, the duty to verify and validate that information is a shared responsibility that every believer must uphold.

The Ethical Imperative: Why We Must Verify

Ethically, the act of verifying religious content is central to maintaining the integrity of one's faith and the faith community at large. Most religious traditions stress the significance of acting with integrity in all aspects of life, and this includes the dissemination of religious knowledge.

- **The Harmful Effects of Misinformation:** Misinformation, particularly when it comes to sacred teachings, can have devastating consequences. It can lead to misinterpretations, confusion, and the perpetuation of false beliefs. For example, in Christianity, spreading incorrect interpretations of scripture can lead people astray, causing confusion about core doctrines. In Islam, the spread of fabricated Hadith or misquoted verses could lead to misguided practices. All faiths are vulnerable to this challenge, making verification not just a personal responsibility but a communal one.
- **A Universal Ethical Duty:** In all major religions, there is an ethical call to speak and act truthfully. This duty includes not only being truthful ourselves but also ensuring that the information we share is accurate and reflective of the sacred texts and traditions. The failure to verify could lead to the spread of false teachings, which in turn can cause harm to individuals' spiritual journeys and disrupt the unity within religious communities.

The Role of Verification in Preserving Sacred Knowledge

Sacred texts and teachings are central to every religious tradition. They offer guidance, wisdom, and a framework for living a moral and virtuous life. Preserving the authenticity of these teachings is paramount, and verification is the key to safeguarding this authenticity in the modern, digital age.

- **Preserving Sacred Knowledge Across Generations:** Religious teachings are passed down through generations, and it is the responsibility of each individual to ensure that these teachings are preserved accurately. In Hinduism, the concept of "Shruti" refers to knowledge that is heard and passed down verbatim. Similarly, in

Islam, the Quran is regarded as the literal word of God, and its preservation is central to Islamic faith. All religions have mechanisms in place to protect the integrity of their sacred texts, and verification is the modern extension of this preservation effort.

- **The Role of Digital Platforms in Protecting Sacred Texts:** With the rise of the internet, sacred texts and teachings are now more accessible than ever. While this democratization of knowledge is a positive development, it also poses challenges in maintaining the accuracy of religious content. Individuals must therefore take the initiative to verify the information they encounter online, ensuring that it remains faithful to the original teachings.

The Consequences of Failing to Verify Religious Content

Failing to verify religious content is not a neutral act—it carries serious consequences. Spreading unverified religious information can distort the original messages, lead to the formation of false beliefs, and even incite discord among religious communities.

- **Spreading Misinformation Leads to Division:** When religious content is shared without proper verification, it can lead to misconceptions and even conflict between different religious groups. For example, misquoted religious texts can fuel interfaith misunderstandings and deepen divides. In times of political or social unrest, misinformation can be particularly dangerous, as it may be used to manipulate religious sentiments for other purposes.
- **Loss of Trust and Faith:** If individuals and communities repeatedly encounter misinformation, they may lose trust in the religious institutions that are responsible for guiding them. This erosion of trust can lead to spiritual disillusionment, questioning the validity of sacred texts, and undermining the unity of faith communities.

A Universal Call for Action: Verification as a Shared Duty

Across all faiths, the importance of verifying religious content is a call to action that transcends individual beliefs. This is not a task for religious scholars alone; it is a shared responsibility for all members of the faith community. It is through collective vigilance that religious communities can ensure the integrity of their sacred knowledge and prevent the spread of misinformation.

- **The Role of Religious Communities:** Religious communities must come together to promote the verification of religious content. This can be achieved by creating platforms for discussing and verifying religious texts, providing access to reliable sources, and fostering interfaith dialogue to share best practices for maintaining accuracy.
- **A Global Responsibility:** The digital age requires global collaboration in preserving the authenticity of religious teachings. Whether through social media, blogs, websites, or other platforms, individuals from all religions must work together to ensure that religious content is accurate and that truth prevails. This will help to maintain the dignity and respect of religious traditions and ensure that sacred knowledge is passed down in its purest form.

Conclusion: A Universal Mandate to Verify Religious Knowledge

Verification is more than a modern need; it is a timeless religious duty shared across faiths. Each believer must take personal responsibility to ensure the accuracy of religious content, recognizing that unchecked misinformation threatens not only individual understanding but also the integrity of sacred knowledge and the unity of spiritual communities. By actively questioning, confirming, and safeguarding what we read and share, people of all traditions can help protect the sanctity of their beliefs and preserve the harmony that binds faith communities together.

4.2 The Responsibility of the User

In a time when religious content is widely available across digital platforms, every individual has an important role in ensuring that the information they consume, share, and contribute to is accurate and trustworthy. This responsibility transcends religious boundaries and calls for a collective effort from all people of faith, regardless of their specific beliefs, to ensure that the digital space remains a place of integrity and truth. Religious teachings from various traditions have long emphasized the value of truth, accountability, and wisdom. These principles are crucial now more than ever as we navigate a world where misinformation can easily spread, especially in matters of faith.

The Universal Responsibility for Verifying Religious Content

Across all faiths, the pursuit of truth is a fundamental tenet. Every individual, as part of their religious duty, must be vigilant about the information they interact with, particularly when it pertains to religious teachings. Whether it's a Christian sharing a Bible verse, a Hindu referencing the Bhagavad Gita, a Buddhist quoting teachings from the Dhammapada, or a Muslim sharing a Hadith, the responsibility to ensure that these teachings are presented accurately falls on each of us.

- **Truth and accountability.** In many religious traditions, truth is sacred. For example, the Bible states, "You shall not bear false witness against your neighbor" (Exodus 20:16). Similarly, in Hinduism, there is an emphasis on "Satyam," the concept of truth, as integral to spiritual life. From a Buddhist perspective, following the Eightfold Path involves right speech, which includes speaking the truth. This universal value means that all religious adherents are called to act as gatekeepers of religious knowledge, ensuring that what is shared is accurate and not distorted.
- **Spreading truth across faiths.** The responsibility of verifying religious content is not limited to one group, as all people who

share religious information should strive to ensure the accuracy of what they communicate. This is especially important in an era where digital platforms allow for rapid dissemination of content, both beneficial and potentially harmful. The content we share must align with the core values of truth upheld by all faiths.

The Dangers of Spreading Misinformation in Religious Contexts

Misinformation related to religion can have far-reaching consequences, affecting both individuals and communities. When false teachings are spread, it can lead to confusion, division, and even harm. The consequences of unverified religious content are particularly severe because they can influence people's beliefs, behaviors, and spiritual practices.

- **Misinterpretations and misunderstandings.** When religious texts or teachings are misquoted, it can result in major misinterpretations that undermine the core messages of peace, compassion, and unity that are central to most religious teachings. For instance, misquoting a sacred text may lead to harmful ideologies or incorrect practices, misleading individuals in their spiritual journeys.
- **Social division.** False religious content can also exacerbate existing divisions between different faith groups. This can contribute to intolerance, extremism, and even violence. Therefore, it is important that users of all faiths are aware of the impact of spreading inaccurate religious content and take active steps to prevent it.
- **Trust and integrity in faith communities.** Trust is essential in any community, and religious communities are no exception. Misinformation erodes this trust and can cause discord among believers. When religious content is shared without verification, it undermines the integrity of both the content and the person sharing it.

The Role of the User as a Steward of Religious Truth

Each individual who shares or consumes religious content online has a responsibility to safeguard its truthfulness. This is a shared duty among all who are part of the digital age, and it involves taking a proactive stance in questioning and verifying information before it is passed on.

- **Checking sources and context.** The first step in fulfilling this responsibility is to evaluate the source of religious content. Is it from a credible and authoritative source within the relevant faith tradition? Has it been presented in its full context, not just a fragment taken out of context? For example, a quote from the Bible, Quran, Torah, or any other religious scripture should be accurately referenced, and its context must be respected to avoid misinterpretation.
- **Using reliable tools and resources.** In the digital age, there are many tools available for verifying information. Fact-checking websites, expert opinions, and authoritative religious scholars can help individuals determine the validity of religious content. By making use of these resources, users can ensure that they are spreading only the most accurate and truthful information.

Ethical Responsibility in Sharing Religious Knowledge

From a universal perspective, ethics plays a vital role in the way religious content is shared. In nearly every faith tradition, ethical teachings are tied to the concept of responsible speech. The act of sharing religious content should not be taken lightly, as it has the power to shape people's beliefs and spiritual practices.

- **The ethical duty to share what is true.** As mentioned in various sacred texts, ethics in communication is a critical aspect of spiritual life. For instance, in Christianity, the Apostle Paul urges believers to "speak the truth in love" (Ephesians 4:15), which emphasizes the importance of sharing truth responsibly. Similarly, the Bhagavad Gita encourages us to avoid actions or speech that mislead others. This universal teaching across religions emphasizes the need for truth to be shared in an ethical, responsible manner.

- **The potential harm of spreading false religious knowledge.** Just as misinformation in other areas can lead to harm, false religious knowledge can have even greater consequences for individuals' faith lives. It can distort one's understanding of sacred teachings and lead to misguided practices. Therefore, it is imperative to evaluate religious content carefully before sharing it, ensuring that it aligns with the core principles of the religion it represents.

A Collective Effort: Maintaining the Integrity of Religious Knowledge

The responsibility of verifying religious content is not only an individual one but a collective effort. All members of religious communities—whether through digital platforms, social media, or direct communication—must join forces to maintain the integrity of religious knowledge. This collective effort helps to ensure that the religious teachings we encounter online reflect the true values and beliefs of our faith traditions.

- **Collaborating for truth across faiths.** Religious communities must work together, sharing tools and resources to help verify religious content. Collaboration among different faith traditions can lead to a more robust understanding of religious texts, shared ethics, and common principles that govern the responsible dissemination of knowledge. For instance, interfaith dialogues can encourage mutual respect for each faith's core tenets while also promoting truth and transparency in the digital space.
- **A united commitment to truth.** Ultimately, the goal is to foster a global community where truth is upheld in all forms of

communication, particularly religious discourse. By working together, individuals from all faiths can ensure that the religious content shared online aligns with the ethical values of honesty, respect, and compassion.

Conclusion: A Universal Call for Responsibility in Sharing Religious Content

In conclusion, the responsibility of verifying religious content is universal, extending beyond any one faith or belief system. It is a shared obligation among all digital citizens to ensure that the religious information we encounter, share, and promote is true and beneficial. As individuals, we must be vigilant in evaluating sources, questioning claims, and verifying facts before passing them on.

By doing so, we fulfill our ethical and spiritual duties to preserve the integrity of religious teachings across all faiths. The consequences of spreading misinformation in religious contexts are far-reaching, affecting both personal faith and the global religious community. Therefore, it is imperative that we take responsibility for the accuracy of the religious content we share, ensuring that the digital world remains a space for truth, respect, and interfaith cooperation.

4.3 The Role of Religious Authorities

In the age of information overload, where everyone with access to the internet can share their interpretations of sacred texts, the role of religious authorities has never been more critical. Religious leaders, scholars, and institutions must step forward as guiding lights in verifying and preserving the authenticity of religious content. Their expertise, grounded in years of study, understanding, and interpretation, provides the foundation for ensuring that the teachings of faith are communicated in their most accurate form. In the absence of such authoritative oversight, misinformation can easily infiltrate the religious discourse, leading followers astray.

The Authority of Religious Scholars and Institutions

Religious authorities have traditionally held the responsibility of interpreting and disseminating sacred texts. They are entrusted with the knowledge and wisdom passed down through generations, and their role in verifying religious information is essential in maintaining the integrity of faith. Whether it's a well-established institution or a respected scholar, religious authorities serve as the custodians of truth, ensuring that the sacred teachings remain intact despite the challenges of modern communication technologies.

- **Traditional Role of Religious Scholars:** Historically, religious scholars have been the primary interpreters of sacred texts. Their deep understanding of religious law, philosophy, and ethics makes them the most reliable sources of religious knowledge. Their interpretations have been vetted through years of study and discussion, giving them the credibility necessary to protect against misinterpretation. This role is essential not only in guiding believers but also in educating them about the proper methods for understanding and applying religious teachings.

- **Modern Role of Religious Institutions:** In today's digital world, religious institutions, such as universities, mosques, churches, synagogues, and temples, continue to play a central role in ensuring the accuracy of religious teachings. These institutions act as intermediaries, helping individuals navigate the overwhelming amount of religious content available online. They offer courses, lectures, and sermons that reflect the authentic understanding of their respective traditions, equipping believers with the tools they need to critically evaluate what they encounter on digital platforms.

The Need for Scholarly Oversight in the Digital Age

The sheer volume of religious content being produced and consumed online today requires constant vigilance and oversight by qualified religious authorities. Without such oversight, the risk of misinterpretation, distortion, and the spread of false teachings is heightened. Religious authorities are not only responsible for verifying content but also for providing context and explanation to ensure that followers understand the deeper meanings behind sacred texts.

- **The Challenge of Unregulated Content:** In the absence of scholarly oversight, anyone can present themselves as a religious expert, often without the necessary qualifications or training. This has led to a rise in self-proclaimed "spiritual influencers" who, despite lacking deep knowledge of the faith, have a wide-reaching impact on their audiences. Without the checks and balances of established religious authorities, these influencers may mislead their followers by offering unverified, superficial, or even harmful interpretations of religious principles.

- **The Need for a Standardized Approach:** To counteract this issue, religious authorities must collaborate to develop a standardized approach to religious content verification. This approach would ensure that teachings remain consistent with the core principles of faith, regardless of how they are presented online. Religious institutions must establish guidelines for evaluating the authenticity of religious content, training individuals to discern credible sources, and developing strategies for combating misinformation.

Facilitating Access to Authentic Religious Knowledge

One of the most valuable contributions that religious authorities can make in the digital age is facilitating easy access to authentic religious knowledge. This can be achieved by ensuring that official platforms, whether websites, apps, or social media pages, provide accurate, reliable, and easily accessible content. By doing so, religious authorities can offer a clear alternative to the flood of unverified and misleading information found online.

- **Official Religious Platforms and Resources:** Religious authorities should be proactive in establishing and maintaining digital platforms that offer accurate interpretations of sacred texts, religious guidance, and educational resources. Websites, mobile apps, and online forums created and maintained by credible religious institutions can provide a trustworthy source of religious knowledge that adheres to the established principles of the faith. These platforms can act as a counterbalance to misinformation, offering users a place to verify teachings and find reliable answers to their questions.
- **Engagement with Digital Communities:** Religious leaders and institutions must also engage directly with digital communities to ensure that they are equipped with the correct knowledge. This could involve hosting online seminars, live discussions, Q&A sessions, and producing high-quality educational videos and articles that directly address common misconceptions or challenges faced by believers. By engaging with digital audiences in these ways, religious authorities can actively shape the narrative and guide the faithful towards the truth.

The Role of Religious Authorities in Educating the Public

In addition to verifying religious content, religious authorities also have the critical role of educating the public about the importance of verifying information. This educational effort should not be limited to formal settings like religious schools or institutions but should also extend to broader outreach through digital media, conferences, and community events.

- **Educational Campaigns on Verification:** Religious authorities can initiate educational campaigns to raise awareness about the risks of misinformation and the importance of verifying religious content before accepting or sharing it. These campaigns can include informational pamphlets, webinars, and community workshops focused on helping individuals identify credible sources and teaching them how to fact-check religious information.
- **Promoting Digital Literacy:** Educating the public about digital literacy is a vital part of helping them navigate the complex digital landscape. Religious authorities should promote the skills necessary for users to critically evaluate the sources of religious content they encounter online. This includes encouraging people to ask questions, seek clarification from trusted scholars, and be cautious of content that lacks clear, verifiable sources.

Building Trust Between Religious Authorities and Digital Users

For religious authorities to effectively guide digital users in verifying religious content, trust is paramount. This trust can only be built through transparency, consistency, and a genuine commitment to preserving the authenticity of the faith. Religious authorities must be open and approachable, demonstrating a willingness to engage with followers on various platforms and address their concerns in a timely and compassionate manner.

- **Transparency in Religious Leadership:** Religious authorities must lead by example, demonstrating transparency in how they engage with digital content and the methods they use to verify it. By sharing their processes for validating information and being open about their sources, they can build credibility and earn the trust of their followers. This transparency will also help demystify the process of religious verification, making it more accessible to the broader community.
- **Ongoing Dialogue and Adaptation:** As digital platforms continue to evolve, religious authorities must remain adaptable, continually learning about new technologies, social media trends, and emerging forms of misinformation. By staying informed and engaged, they can ensure that they are providing up-to-date guidance on how to navigate the ever-changing digital landscape.

Conclusion: The Essential Role of Religious Authorities in Protecting Sacred Knowledge

In conclusion, religious authorities play a crucial role in the verification and dissemination of sacred knowledge in the digital age. Through their expertise, they serve as protectors of religious integrity, ensuring that the teachings of faith are not distorted or diluted by misinformation. By actively engaging with digital platforms, educating the public on verification methods, and providing transparent and reliable sources of religious content, religious authorities can safeguard the authenticity of sacred knowledge for future generations. This will help foster a more informed, spiritually grounded, and united community of believers, regardless of the digital challenges they may face.

4.4 Best Practices for Ensuring Authenticity

In the era of digital information, where religious knowledge is freely available but also prone to distortion, adopting best practices for verifying content has become a necessity for believers of all faiths. Ensuring the authenticity of religious teachings and texts is essential not only to protect the integrity of sacred traditions but also to prevent the spread of false information. By following specific best practices, individuals, communities, and religious institutions can work together to maintain the purity of religious content while navigating the complexities of the digital world.

Relying on Trusted Sources

The foundation of verifying religious content lies in identifying and relying on trusted sources. Sacred texts, interpretations, and religious guidance should always come from those who have the necessary credentials and expertise. Trusted sources include recognized religious authorities, established religious institutions, and scholars with years of academic training and practical experience in the interpretation of sacred texts.

- **Scriptures and Authorized Translations:** When referring to sacred scriptures, it is essential to use officially authorized translations and editions. These texts, which have undergone rigorous scholarly review and are often accompanied by footnotes, commentaries, and references, ensure that the original meaning and intent of the scriptures are preserved. Whenever possible, readers should consult these primary sources rather than secondary or unofficial versions, as discrepancies and inaccuracies may arise in unverified publications.
- **Scholarly Expertise and Institutional Oversight:** Reputable scholars and religious institutions are indispensable in ensuring that religious content is consistent with the tradition's core

teachings. Their deep understanding of theology, historical context, and religious philosophy positions them to offer authoritative interpretations. It is important to seek guidance from scholars who have received formal training in the subject matter and are affiliated with recognized religious institutions, which helps safeguard the credibility and accuracy of their teachings.

Cross-Referencing Information

One of the most effective ways to verify religious content is through cross-referencing. This involves comparing information from multiple credible sources to ensure consistency and accuracy. Cross-referencing is especially useful when encountering content that seems unfamiliar, controversial, or too advanced for personal understanding. By seeking out diverse perspectives on the same topic, individuals can better understand the nuances and complexities of religious texts and teachings.

- **Comparing Multiple Versions of Sacred Texts:** For individuals seeking to understand specific verses or passages, it is valuable to consult various interpretations or translations of sacred scriptures. Different schools of thought may offer varying interpretations of a text, and understanding these interpretations helps prevent misinterpretation. For example, consulting different translations of the Quran, the Bible, or the Torah can provide a fuller understanding of a passage's meaning.
- **Consulting Multiple Scholars and Opinions:** In many religious traditions, there is not just one interpretation of a text. Religious scholars often offer diverse perspectives, shaped by different historical, cultural, and theological contexts. By consulting multiple scholars or religious figures, believers can gain a more comprehensive understanding of complex teachings. This is particularly important in cases where a text or concept has multiple

layers of meaning or where there are disagreements about its interpretation.

Verifying with Religious Communities

While individual verification is essential, the communal aspect of religious practice also plays a role in verifying content. Religious communities—whether local congregations, study groups, or online forums—offer an invaluable resource for mutual verification. By engaging in discussions, asking questions, and sharing insights, believers can collaboratively ensure that the religious knowledge they are accessing aligns with the true teachings of their faith.

- **Community Discussions and Study Groups:** Religious study groups provide an environment where individuals can come together to discuss and verify the authenticity of religious content. These gatherings, whether in person or online, foster an atmosphere of collaboration, where believers can share insights, clarify doubts, and cross-check information. Study groups led by knowledgeable religious figures or scholars are especially valuable, as they provide access to the wisdom of those with deep theological expertise.

- **Religious Forums and Online Platforms:** Online religious forums and platforms offer a space for individuals from different regions and backgrounds to engage in discussions about religious topics. These platforms can act as a collaborative environment for verification, where individuals can pose questions, share resources, and seek guidance from others. However, it is crucial to choose reputable forums with active moderation, where qualified experts can guide the discussions and ensure that misinformation is corrected.

Fact-Checking Tools and Technologies

In addition to traditional methods of verification, there are a growing number of fact-checking tools and technologies available that can assist in verifying religious content. These tools are especially useful when it comes to ensuring the accuracy of information found online. Many of these tools leverage advanced algorithms, AI, and crowdsourcing to identify discrepancies, false claims, or misquotes in religious content.

- **AI-Powered Fact-Checking Tools:** There are now AI-based fact-checking platforms that can quickly identify misinformation and cross-check content across the web. These platforms analyze vast amounts of data and compare information against credible sources to identify inconsistencies or inaccuracies. By using these tools, individuals and religious institutions can more effectively verify religious content before sharing or disseminating it.
- **Crowdsourced Verification Platforms:** Some online platforms allow users to submit content for peer review, where fellow users can flag potential misinformation. These platforms leverage the collective knowledge of a large number of users to verify the authenticity of religious content. While crowdsourced platforms can be effective, they require active moderation to ensure that the verification process is accurate and unbiased.

Promoting Digital Literacy and Critical Thinking

Religious leaders and scholars must encourage digital literacy and critical thinking within their communities. By promoting these skills, believers will be better equipped to navigate the digital age and discern truth from falsehood. Digital literacy is not just about knowing how to use technology; it's about understanding how to evaluate sources, identify biases, and critically engage with the information presented.

- **Teaching Critical Thinking in Religious Education:** Religious institutions should include critical thinking as a key component of their educational curricula. This includes teaching believers how to approach religious content with a discerning eye, question its authenticity, and analyze its alignment with the core teachings of their faith. By fostering critical thinking, religious authorities can empower their followers to take responsibility for verifying the religious content they encounter.
- **Encouraging Media Literacy:** Alongside critical thinking, media literacy is crucial in today's digital environment. Believers must be taught how to identify reliable sources of information, understand the potential for manipulation or bias in digital media, and learn how to fact-check content before trusting or sharing it. Religious communities can host workshops, webinars, and seminars to teach these essential skills, ensuring that individuals are well-equipped to navigate the complex world of online religious discourse.

Conclusion: A Collective Responsibility to Preserve Authenticity

In conclusion, ensuring the authenticity of religious content in the digital age requires a multifaceted approach that combines traditional methods of verification with modern tools and technologies. By relying on trusted sources, cross-referencing information, engaging with religious communities, and leveraging fact-checking tools, believers can protect the integrity of sacred knowledge. Moreover, by promoting digital literacy and critical thinking, religious authorities can empower individuals to take responsibility for verifying the religious content they encounter. The collective effort of religious leaders, scholars, and the community will ensure that religious teachings remain pure and accurate for generations to come, fostering a more informed and spiritually grounded society.

Chapter 5: Solutions — AI to Be Handled with Care

5.1 The Need for AI Collaboration with Religious Experts

As artificial intelligence (AI) continues to evolve, it becomes increasingly important to acknowledge its growing role in the digital dissemination of religious knowledge. However, AI, no matter how sophisticated, lacks the depth, sensitivity, and understanding of sacred texts that human experts bring to the table. This gap in comprehension raises an essential question: how can AI and religious scholars collaborate to maintain the integrity of religious content while embracing the benefits of technology?

AI offers unprecedented opportunities for scaling the accessibility of religious teachings. It allows people from diverse geographical locations to access teachings and sacred texts from various religious traditions. However, given the potential for misinformation, AI must be integrated thoughtfully and cautiously into the domain of religious knowledge. This calls for a partnership between AI and religious experts who are equipped with the proper knowledge and authority to ensure that the technology serves as a tool for promoting truth, rather than a vehicle for error.

Human Oversight of AI-Generated Religious Content

AI systems, such as machine learning algorithms and natural language processing models, are capable of generating religious content at an astounding pace. These systems can analyze massive amounts of text and data, which makes them useful for certain tasks, such as organizing information, providing summaries, or identifying patterns within large datasets. However, when it comes to religious knowledge—an area deeply rooted in human interpretation, cultural context, and spiritual insight—AI needs the oversight of qualified religious scholars to ensure accuracy and avoid misrepresentation.

- **The Role of Religious Scholars:** Religious scholars possess an understanding of sacred texts, historical context, and theological principles that AI systems cannot replicate. By working in collaboration with AI, scholars can oversee the generated content, ensuring it adheres to the correct interpretations of religious scriptures. This partnership can also prevent AI from making mistakes, which might otherwise lead to misinterpretation or even distortion of sacred teachings.
- **AI as a Tool, not a Replacement:** AI should not be seen as a replacement for human expertise in religious matters. Instead, it can serve as a powerful tool that enhances the work of scholars and religious educators. For example, AI can be used to quickly analyze different interpretations of religious texts, but religious scholars should play the final role in ensuring these interpretations align with the true teachings of their respective faiths.

Collaborative Creation of AI Training Data

One of the challenges of implementing AI in the realm of religious knowledge is ensuring that the data it is trained on is authentic and reflects the full depth of religious understanding. To achieve this, collaboration between AI developers and religious scholars is crucial in creating a training dataset that accurately represents the diversity of thought within religious traditions.

- **Inclusive Representation of Religious Diversity:** Religions, by nature, are diverse, with different sects, schools of thought, and interpretations of sacred texts. AI must be trained on data that reflects this diversity to avoid bias and to ensure that content generated by AI does not lean towards a particular interpretation. This requires collaboration between scholars from various religious traditions to compile a comprehensive and balanced dataset.

- **Ensuring Textual Accuracy and Contextual Integrity:** Religious texts and teachings often have multiple layers of meaning, which can vary depending on the context in which they are interpreted. For AI to accurately interpret these texts, religious scholars must ensure that the data it is trained on includes accurate and contextually appropriate interpretations. This will prevent AI from making oversimplified or incorrect readings of complex religious doctrines.

AI-Assisted Verification Tools for Religious Content

In addition to generating religious content, AI can also play a vital role in verifying the authenticity of content. AI-assisted verification tools can help religious communities and scholars identify discrepancies, errors, and potentially misleading information. By collaborating with experts, AI can be used to cross-check information across a wide range of sources and flag content that is inconsistent with authoritative interpretations of religious teachings.

- **AI-Powered Fact-Checking Systems:** Fact-checking is an essential part of ensuring the authenticity of religious content. AI systems can quickly analyze large volumes of religious content, comparing it against verified texts, translations, and interpretations. These systems can identify inconsistencies or misquotes and alert users to potential inaccuracies. While human oversight is still needed to make final decisions, AI-assisted verification tools can significantly streamline the process.
- **Automated Monitoring of Religious Content:** AI can also be used to monitor religious content on digital platforms and websites, identifying and flagging content that may not align with accepted religious teachings. This proactive approach helps prevent misinformation from spreading and ensures that only verified content is shared with the wider public. Religious experts and scholars can collaborate with AI developers to create a system

that accurately monitors digital content while preserving the integrity of religious teachings.

Ethical Considerations in AI-Religious Collaboration

The collaboration between AI and religious experts is not without its ethical challenges. As AI becomes more integrated into religious content creation and verification, it is essential to consider the ethical implications of such collaboration. These considerations must address concerns about privacy, bias, and the potential for misuse.

- **Bias in AI Systems:** AI systems are not inherently neutral; they can inherit biases present in the data they are trained on. These biases can influence the way AI processes and interprets religious content. To address this issue, scholars must work with AI developers to identify and mitigate biases in the training data and ensure that AI systems process religious texts in a way that reflects the diverse range of interpretations within religious traditions.
- **Privacy and Data Security:** Religious content is deeply personal, and individuals may have concerns about how their interactions with AI systems are monitored or stored. It is essential for AI developers to ensure that privacy and data security are maintained when AI is used in religious contexts. Clear guidelines should be established to protect individuals' personal information while using AI systems to access or verify religious content.
- **Ethical Use of AI in Religious Contexts:** As AI plays a greater role in shaping religious discourse, it is important to establish ethical guidelines that govern how AI is used. These guidelines should ensure that AI is used in ways that are consistent with the ethical principles of the religion in question and that it does not lead to the exploitation or manipulation of religious followers.

Empowering Religious Organizations through Technology for Content Verification

As artificial intelligence (AI) continues to redefine the landscape of information dissemination, it is crucial for leading religious organizations to not only adapt but actively take charge in shaping the digital era of religious knowledge.

- **Developing Robust Online Platforms:** By developing robust online platforms—such as chatbots, mobile apps, and dedicated websites—religious institutions can provide their followers with accessible, accurate, and real-time tools for verifying religious content. These platforms will allow users to easily cross-check religious teachings, ensuring they align with authentic interpretations of sacred texts.
- **AI-Powered Verification with Human Oversight:** These platforms can integrate AI-powered verification systems that allow users to cross-check religious teachings. Additionally, they could offer a combination of automated fact-checking tools and human oversight from religious scholars, ensuring a balance between technology and traditional knowledge.
- **Creating Seamless, Trustworthy Alternatives:** Just as AI platforms are becoming the go-to source for general information, religious organizations can set a precedent by offering a seamless, trustworthy alternative for verifying religious content. With accessible interfaces and multilingual support, these platforms can become essential tools for religious communities worldwide.
- **Fostering Engagement and Ethical AI Use:** Beyond verification, these platforms could also offer educational resources on how to engage with AI responsibly. This approach would foster a deeper connection between followers and their faith while empowering them to discern truth from distortion in the digital space.

Building a Sustainable Framework for Collaboration

The collaboration between AI and religious experts must be built on a sustainable and mutually beneficial framework. This framework should prioritize the accuracy, authenticity, and ethical integrity of religious content, while also embracing the opportunities that AI can offer for disseminating religious teachings to a global audience.

- **Long-Term Partnerships:** Successful collaboration between AI developers and religious scholars will require long-term partnerships based on trust, transparency, and shared goals. Religious institutions and AI developers must work together to create systems that respect religious traditions while using technology to improve access to knowledge and promote spiritual growth.
- **Ongoing Education and Training:** As AI continues to evolve, religious experts must stay informed about technological advancements and learn how to effectively integrate AI into their work. This may involve ongoing training and education for religious leaders, scholars, and institutions to ensure that they can effectively navigate the challenges and opportunities presented by AI.

Conclusion: A Harmonious Integration of Technology and Spirituality

By combining AI with scholarly oversight, ethical frameworks, and inclusive data, religious communities can responsibly harness technology to protect authenticity and combat misinformation. This partnership helps keep sacred knowledge pure and accessible, ensuring it stays relevant and meaningful for future generations while deepening collective spiritual understanding.

5.2 Technological Solutions for Verification

In an age dominated by information overload, verifying the authenticity of religious content becomes a critical issue. Artificial intelligence (AI) holds the promise of transforming the way we assess the credibility of information, especially in the context of sacred knowledge. However, in order to effectively harness this potential, it is crucial to develop and implement technological solutions that focus on verifying the accuracy and authenticity of religious content. This topic will explore how AI can be used as a tool for verification and highlight the various technological solutions available to ensure that religious information is both accurate and trustworthy.

AI-Powered Fact-Checking Tools

One of the most important technological solutions AI can offer is the development of advanced fact-checking systems. These systems are designed to verify the authenticity of statements, quotes, and texts by cross-referencing them with authoritative sources. In the case of religious texts, AI-powered fact-checking tools can be trained to compare religious quotes, teachings, and interpretations against established and trusted references such as scriptures, theological commentaries, and consensus statements from religious authorities.

- **Automated Cross-Referencing:** AI fact-checking systems can perform cross-referencing across various texts, databases, and online resources to quickly verify the authenticity of a religious quote or claim. This can significantly speed up the process of verifying content, ensuring that religious teachings shared in public domains are reliable and not misleading. By automating the comparison process, these tools can help reduce human error and bias in the verification process.
- **Identifying Misinformation and Misquotations:** AI systems can be trained to detect common patterns of misinformation and

misquotations that often circulate in religious communities. These systems can flag discrepancies between what is being claimed and what is found in the original source texts. By identifying and correcting such errors, AI can play an instrumental role in preventing the spread of false information that may distort religious teachings.

Blockchain Technology for Data Integrity

Another technological solution for ensuring the authenticity of religious content is the use of blockchain technology. Blockchain is a decentralized, tamper-resistant ledger that can be used to verify the provenance and integrity of digital content. By utilizing blockchain, religious institutions and scholars can create a system that tracks the origin and modifications of religious texts and content, providing a transparent record of how the content has been shared, edited, and updated over time.

- **Immutable Records:** Blockchain technology provides an immutable record of data, meaning once a piece of information is recorded, it cannot be altered without leaving a trace. This feature can be leveraged to track the history of religious texts, ensuring that the original versions of sacred writings remain intact and unmodified. This is particularly important for preserving the accuracy of religious content and preventing tampering or deliberate alterations.
- **Verification of Sources:** Blockchain can also be used to authenticate the sources of religious content. Each piece of religious information can be traced back to its original source through blockchain-based records, allowing users to verify that the content they are consuming is credible and has not been altered or misrepresented. This solution helps to build trust in the dissemination of religious knowledge, particularly in digital formats.

Natural Language Processing (NLP) for Contextual Understanding

Natural Language Processing (NLP), a subset of AI, plays a crucial role in helping AI systems understand and interpret the meaning behind religious texts. NLP algorithms can analyze the context in which words and phrases are used, allowing AI to interpret the nuances of sacred knowledge in a more accurate and context-sensitive manner. This capability is essential for verifying religious content, as sacred texts are often complex and require a deep understanding of historical, linguistic, and cultural context.

- **Contextual Analysis of Religious Texts:** NLP models can be trained to recognize and interpret the contextual meaning of religious scriptures. This is important for ensuring that AI does not misquote or misinterpret texts due to a lack of understanding of context. By analyzing the surrounding text and historical background, AI can provide more accurate interpretations of religious content, ensuring that sacred knowledge is conveyed as intended by religious authorities.
- **Semantic Verification:** NLP can also be used to perform semantic verification, ensuring that religious content is consistent with the intended theological meaning. AI systems can compare the meanings of different phrases, words, or sentences within a given text, checking whether they align with recognized interpretations of religious teachings. This process helps to prevent misrepresentations and ensures that AI-generated content reflects the true meaning of sacred texts.

AI-Driven Semantic Search Engines

AI-driven semantic search engines are another valuable tool for verifying religious content. Unlike traditional search engines that focus on keywords, semantic search engines focus on the meaning and context of the search query. These search engines use advanced AI algorithms to analyze and understand the intent behind a user's query, providing more accurate and relevant results.

- **Accurate Content Retrieval:** AI-powered semantic search engines can help religious scholars and content consumers quickly locate trustworthy religious texts and authoritative interpretations. By analyzing the user's query and comparing it against a database of verified religious sources, these search engines can provide users with reliable and contextually appropriate information. This reduces the risk of encountering misquoted or inaccurate content.
- **Reducing Misinformation:** AI-driven search engines can also be used to filter out unreliable sources of information. By focusing on credible, verified religious texts and authoritative commentaries, these systems can help users avoid content that is inaccurate or misleading. This is especially important in the digital age, where misinformation can spread quickly and easily.

AI-Enabled Monitoring Systems for Digital Content

To further combat the spread of misinformation, AI-enabled monitoring systems can be deployed to track religious content across digital platforms and social media. These systems can scan websites, blogs, social media posts, and online forums to identify potential instances of misquoted or misrepresented religious content.

- **Real-Time Detection and Alerts:** AI-powered monitoring systems can work in real time, scanning vast amounts of online content for potential inaccuracies or misquotations. When suspicious content is detected, these systems can alert religious authorities, scholars, or moderators, enabling them to quickly intervene and correct the misinformation before it spreads further.
- **Crowdsourced Verification:** AI monitoring systems can also be integrated with crowdsourced verification tools, where users can report and flag questionable content. This collaborative approach

allows religious communities to work together to identify and correct misinformation, ensuring that only accurate and authentic religious knowledge is shared online.

Conclusion: Leveraging Technology to Safeguard Religious Knowledge

As AI continues to advance, technological solutions for verifying religious content will become increasingly vital in preserving the authenticity and integrity of sacred knowledge. From AI-powered fact-checking tools to blockchain technology, natural language processing, and semantic search engines, there are numerous ways in which AI can be harnessed to ensure that religious teachings remain accurate and trustworthy. However, these technologies must be used in conjunction with human oversight and collaboration with religious experts to maintain the ethical and theological standards of sacred knowledge. By leveraging these technological solutions, religious communities can safeguard the integrity of their teachings while embracing the benefits of AI, ensuring that future generations have access to authentic and reliable religious content.

5.3 Raising Awareness

In the digital age, where information is created and shared at an unprecedented pace, raising awareness about the importance of verifying religious content becomes not only necessary but urgent. The potential risks of misinformation in the realm of sacred knowledge are significant, as they can lead to confusion, misinterpretation, and, in some cases, harm to faith communities. As we embrace the power of AI and technology in disseminating religious content, it is equally important to emphasize the responsibility of individuals, religious institutions, and society at large to raise awareness about the dangers of misinformation and the importance of preserving the authenticity of religious knowledge.

Educating Religious Leaders and Scholars

The first line of defense against misinformation is the religious leadership itself. Religious leaders, scholars, and educators must be equipped with the knowledge and skills necessary to understand the complexities of AI and its potential impact on religious content. By educating those who play an authoritative role in interpreting religious teachings, we can ensure that they are prepared to guide their communities in a world where digital misinformation can easily spread.

- **Incorporating AI into Religious Training:** Religious institutions and educational bodies must consider incorporating AI-related training into their curricula. This would not only familiarize religious leaders with the benefits of AI but also equip them with the critical thinking skills required to discern when digital content is accurate or manipulated. Knowledge of AI's strengths and limitations will allow these leaders to make informed decisions when using or endorsing digital platforms for religious teachings.

- **The Role of Religious Scholars in Verification:** Religious scholars are tasked with interpreting and explaining sacred texts. Their role in verifying religious content in the digital space is crucial. Encouraging them to engage with technological solutions such as AI-powered verification tools can empower them to better uphold the authenticity of religious knowledge, ensuring that any content shared by religious institutions is credible and in line with established theological teachings.

Community Engagement and Public Awareness Campaigns

While religious scholars and leaders play an essential role in verifying religious content, the responsibility to raise awareness extends beyond institutions and experts. Communities, both online and offline, must be encouraged to engage critically with the content they encounter. Public awareness campaigns can be a powerful tool in encouraging individuals to question the authenticity of the information they receive, particularly when it pertains to sacred texts and teachings.

- **Promoting Critical Thinking and Media Literacy:** One of the most effective ways to combat misinformation is by teaching people how to think critically about the information they encounter. Media literacy programs, particularly in religious communities, should focus on helping individuals discern between credible sources and unreliable ones. By emphasizing the importance of verifying religious content before sharing it, communities can create a culture of accountability and responsibility when it comes to digital knowledge.
- **Raising Awareness About the Dangers of Blind Trust:** It is crucial to communicate to the public that blind trust in digital platforms—whether AI-powered or human-run—is a risky approach when dealing with sacred knowledge. Misinformation can propagate quickly, and once it enters the public sphere, it becomes difficult to retract. Public awareness campaigns should

emphasize the need for individuals to question and verify before believing or spreading religious content, especially in light of AI's limitations and potential for error.

Collaboration Between Religious Institutions and Tech Developers

To raise awareness effectively, religious institutions must also engage with the very technology developers who are creating AI tools for content creation and dissemination. Collaboration between religious scholars and AI experts can help bridge the gap between the sacred and the digital, ensuring that AI is used responsibly in the context of religious teachings.

- **Establishing Ethical Guidelines for AI in Religious Contexts:** By collaborating with AI developers, religious institutions can help create ethical guidelines for the use of technology in religious contexts. These guidelines should focus on ensuring that AI algorithms respect the sacredness of religious knowledge, prioritize accuracy, and avoid potential biases in the interpretation of sacred texts. Establishing such guidelines will allow both religious institutions and tech developers to work together in promoting the responsible use of AI for the preservation of religious authenticity.
- **Shared Responsibility for Religious Content:** It is essential for both religious authorities and tech developers to recognize their shared responsibility in preserving the integrity of sacred knowledge. Religious institutions can help tech developers understand the nuances of religious teachings and texts, while developers can assist religious leaders in utilizing AI tools to enhance the accuracy and accessibility of religious content. This collaborative approach will strengthen efforts to ensure that digital religious information remains authentic and trustworthy.

Encouraging the Development of AI Solutions with Ethical and Religious Oversight

As AI technology continues to advance, it is crucial that the development of AI solutions for religious content is guided by ethical and religious oversight. Encouraging the development of AI tools with input from religious experts ensures that the technology aligns with the values and principles of various faith traditions.

- **AI Tools Tailored to Religious Contexts:** Developers should be encouraged to create AI tools that are specifically designed to handle religious content, incorporating both ethical and religious considerations. These tools should be trained on authoritative religious texts and interpretive sources, ensuring that AI does not distort the meanings of sacred teachings. Religious oversight during the development phase will ensure that the AI systems remain aligned with the theological teachings of different faiths.
- **Ethical AI Development:** AI tools for religious content should adhere to the highest ethical standards, ensuring that they promote respect, integrity, and accuracy in handling sacred knowledge. This includes ensuring transparency in how AI systems operate, providing clear guidelines for their use, and continuously monitoring their impact on religious communities. Ethical development and oversight will safeguard the authenticity of religious knowledge in an increasingly digital world.

Empowering Individuals to Verify Content

Finally, individuals must be empowered to take responsibility for verifying the religious content they encounter. The tools and knowledge necessary for verification should not be confined to religious institutions or experts alone. Instead, there should be a collective effort to ensure that all individuals are equipped with the skills to verify and question the authenticity of religious teachings in the digital space.

- **Encouraging Self-Verification:** Individuals should be encouraged to verify the content they come across before sharing it with others. By providing access to reliable tools and resources for verification, individuals can become active participants in preserving the accuracy and authenticity of religious knowledge. This can include providing educational resources about how to use AI verification tools, cross-reference religious texts, and evaluate the credibility of digital sources.
- **Creating a Culture of Verification:** A culture of verification should be cultivated within religious communities. This culture would encourage members to actively engage in verifying content before sharing it, fostering a sense of responsibility toward maintaining the authenticity of sacred knowledge. By making verification a common practice, communities can protect themselves from the spread of misinformation while ensuring that only trustworthy religious content is shared and disseminated.

Conclusion: Raising Awareness as a Collective Effort

Raising awareness about the importance of verifying religious content in the digital age is a critical step in ensuring that sacred knowledge remains authentic and accurate. By educating religious leaders, engaging communities, collaborating with tech developers, and empowering individuals, we can create a global effort to preserve the integrity of religious teachings. In the face of rapid technological advancements and the proliferation of misinformation, it is imperative that we recognize the shared responsibility of individuals, religious institutions, and AI developers in safeguarding the authenticity of religious knowledge. Only through collective efforts can we ensure that the truth of sacred teachings is preserved for future generations.

5.4 Practical Steps for Individuals

In the pursuit of preserving the integrity of sacred knowledge in an age dominated by digital technology, individuals have an indispensable role to play. As consumers, sharers, and creators of religious content, it is critical that each person takes responsibility for the information they encounter and disseminate. AI-powered tools, while valuable, can be prone to errors and misinformation. Thus, individuals must actively participate in the verification process to ensure that the sacred texts and teachings they engage with are accurate and authentic.

Developing a Mindset of Critical Engagement

The first practical step for individuals is to adopt a mindset of critical engagement with all content—especially religious content—encountered online. This requires individuals to question and evaluate the sources of information they come across, rather than simply accepting or sharing it without verification. In a world where AI can quickly generate and distribute information, a healthy skepticism is essential to ensuring that only reliable and truthful content is propagated.

- **Be Proactive in Seeking Authoritative Sources:** Individuals must prioritize sourcing religious content from reputable and authoritative sources. This means turning to recognized religious institutions, scholars, and well-established platforms known for their accuracy and integrity. Many online platforms, however, are not regulated for credibility, so it is crucial for individuals to be cautious when engaging with information from unfamiliar or dubious sources.

- **Cross-Reference Information:** When encountering religious content, individuals should cross-reference information from multiple sources. If a particular verse or teaching is being quoted, verify it against trusted religious texts, whether through a digital database, scholarly publications, or reliable online religious institutions. By doing so, individuals can better understand the context and ensure that the message remains authentic.

Utilizing AI Verification Tools

The increasing use of AI in content creation and dissemination necessitates the development and use of AI verification tools. These tools are designed to check the accuracy of digital content, ensuring that religious information is consistent with authentic sources. Individuals can leverage these tools to minimize the risk of misinformation and to make informed decisions when consuming religious content.

- **Adopt AI Tools Designed for Religious Content:** Several AI tools have been developed specifically for verifying religious texts, providing checks on the accuracy of quoted verses, hadith, and religious interpretations. By utilizing such AI systems, individuals can identify errors or misquotes before they are propagated in their own communities. These tools are especially important when content is generated by algorithms, which may not understand the nuanced context of sacred teachings.
- **Stay Informed About Emerging Technologies:** As AI continues to evolve, individuals must stay informed about the latest developments in AI verification tools. Many technological solutions are updated frequently, improving their efficiency and accuracy. Subscribing to relevant updates and news can help individuals access the most effective verification systems available.

Engaging in Community Discussions and Debates

Religious content is not only a matter of personal belief but also a communal experience. Engaging in open discussions within religious communities about the authenticity of religious knowledge is an important step in ensuring that misinformation does not spread.

Through collaborative conversations, individuals can benefit from the collective wisdom of their communities, share insights, and work together to address potential misinformation.

- **Encourage Group Discussions on Digital Content:** Religious communities should host discussions, both online and offline, to critically assess the content that members share or encounter. These discussions can focus on verifying the authenticity of specific teachings, as well as educating individuals on the importance of checking information before sharing it.
- **Use Social Media Responsibly:** Social media platforms are now central to the dissemination of religious content. However, misinformation can spread rapidly through these channels. Individuals should be cautious when sharing religious content on social media, ensuring that it comes from a verified and reliable source. Social media can also serve as a platform for educating others about the importance of authenticity and verification in religious teachings.

Promoting Digital Literacy and Education

To ensure a wide-reaching impact, it is essential for individuals to promote digital literacy within their own communities. Religious content should be shared with the understanding that the digital realm is rife with both legitimate and misleading information. Educating others on how to evaluate online content critically can help prevent the spread of misinformation and uphold the authenticity of religious teachings.

- **Teach Media Literacy in Religious Settings:** Religious institutions should consider incorporating media literacy into their educational programs. By teaching members how to critically evaluate the sources and accuracy of information, these institutions can prepare individuals to be more discerning in their consumption of religious content, both online and offline. Media literacy should focus on recognizing bias, understanding context, and verifying sources.

- **Develop Training Programs for Young People:** Young people are often the most active users of digital platforms and the most vulnerable to misinformation. Religious leaders and educators should develop programs aimed at teaching younger generations how to engage responsibly with religious content in the digital space. These programs can include workshops, seminars, and online courses to develop skills for verifying information, understanding the ethical implications of sharing content, and using AI tools responsibly.

Supporting the Development of Ethical AI

Individuals can also play an essential role in advocating for the development of ethical AI tools that prioritize the authenticity and accuracy of religious content. By supporting organizations, developers, and platforms that focus on ethical AI practices, individuals can contribute to the creation of technologies that safeguard the integrity of sacred knowledge in the digital age.

- **Advocate for Ethical AI in Religious Contexts:** Individuals should voice their support for AI tools and platforms that align with ethical principles and work in harmony with religious values. Encouraging the development of AI systems that respect the sacred nature of religious texts will help create a future where technology and faith coexist in a responsible and ethical manner.
- **Support Religious Institutions in AI Initiatives:** Religious institutions can benefit from individuals who advocate for collaboration with AI developers. Support for such initiatives can include financial backing, promoting awareness of ethical AI projects, or volunteering expertise in both technology and religion. By actively participating in these efforts, individuals help shape the

future of AI in religious contexts and ensure that it remains a tool for truth and authenticity.

Conclusion: Empowering Individuals for Responsible Engagement

The responsibility of safeguarding religious knowledge does not fall solely on institutions or AI developers. Individuals, too, play a pivotal role in ensuring that the sacred texts and teachings they encounter in the digital age remain accurate and authentic. By adopting a mindset of critical engagement, utilizing verification tools, promoting community discussions, and advocating for ethical AI development, individuals can contribute to a global effort to preserve the integrity of religious knowledge. In an era where misinformation is rampant, the collective effort of informed and responsible individuals is crucial in maintaining the authenticity of the world's sacred teachings.

Final Conclusion: Faith, Technology, and Truth

We are no longer just readers, learners, or seekers. We are gatekeepers of truth in an age where convenience can so easily overshadow authenticity. This book has not merely explored the technical clash between artificial intelligence and religious knowledge—it has exposed a deeper crisis: **the quiet erosion of truth under the weight of speed, simplicity, and surface-level understanding**.

Technology, especially AI, has given us instant access to a universe of information. But within that convenience lies a hidden cost—**the loss of depth, accuracy, and sacred responsibility**. Religion is not a content category. It is not a string of quotes to be summarized by a bot. It is a centuries-old trust passed down in ink, in breath, in memory, and in the burning sincerity of those who lived and died preserving it.

Artificial intelligence can assist, but it cannot comprehend. It can generate, but it cannot revere. And when we turn to it blindly, we risk not only misinformation—we risk **misdirection**, the kind that changes the course of faith itself.

That is why the **Golden Rule of Intellectual Integrity** must guide us forward:

"No convenience is worth the cost of truthfulness and authenticity."

This rule is not a suggestion—it is a warning and a standard. In a world addicted to shortcuts, we must be the ones who choose the harder, slower, truer path—because the sacred deserves no less.

Let this book be more than a critique. Let it be a call. A call to religious leaders to rise, not retreat. A call to scholars to collaborate, not compete. A call to technologists to approach with reverence, not arrogance. And a call to every reader to ask: *Is this true? Who said it? And does it honor the weight of divine knowledge?*

The future does not have to be a battleground between faith and innovation. It can be a space where the two meet—on the condition that **truth leads and technology follows**.

You are now among the few who understand the stakes. So carry this awareness, wield it with humility, and whenever AI offers you the easy answer, remember:

Truth is worth the work.

And **authenticity is worth the wait.**

Appendix A: Trusted Sources for Verifying Religious Knowledge

---

In an age of widespread misinformation and AI-generated religious errors, the need to access **authentic, trustworthy sources** has never been greater. Whether you prefer websites or mobile apps, the following list includes **verified platforms across all major religions**, making it easier to **fact-check, study, and grow spiritually** with confidence.

Islam

Websites:

- Quran.com – Authentic Quranic text with translations and tafsir.
- Sunnah.com – Primary Hadith collections with references.
- IslamQA.info – Verified fatwas and scholarly opinions.
- Dar al-Ifta al-Misriyyah – Official fatwa platform.
- Yaqeen Institute – Research-driven Islamic insights.

Mobile Apps:

- **Quran Majeed** (Android / iOS) – High-quality recitations, translations, and tafsir.
- **Muslim Pro** (Android / iOS) – Quran, prayer times, Qibla, and Hadith.
- **Islam 360** (Android / iOS) – Quran with tafsir, Hadith collections, and search features.
- **Hadith Collection** (Android / iOS) – Access to Sahih Bukhari, Muslim, etc.

- **SeekersGuidance** (Android / iOS) – Audio courses, fatwas, and guidance.

Christianity

Websites:

- BibleGateway.com – Read and study multiple Bible versions.
- Blue Letter Bible – Lexicons, interlinear tools.
- Vatican.va – Official Catholic teachings and documents.

Mobile Apps:

- **YouVersion Bible App** (Android / iOS) – Multiple Bible translations, devotionals.
- **Logos Bible Study App** (Android / iOS) – Deep theological tools and commentaries.
- **Daily Bible** (Android / iOS) – Verse of the day, audio Bible, bookmarks.
- **Catholic Daily Readings** (Android / iOS) – Missal, reflections, and liturgical calendar.

Judaism

Websites:

- Sefaria.org – Extensive library of Jewish texts with commentary.
- Chabad.org – Torah study, halachic rulings, Jewish life.

Mobile Apps:

- **Sefaria** (Android / iOS) – Access Tanakh, Talmud, Midrash, and more.
- **Chabad.org App** (Android / iOS) – Articles, Torah study, mitzvah reminders.
- **PocketTorah** (Android / iOS) – Learn Torah portions with audio and Hebrew text.

Hinduism

Websites:

- Sacred-Texts.com (Hinduism)
- Vedabase.io – Vedic texts and commentaries.

Mobile Apps:

- **Bhagavad Gita – Hindi & English** (Android / iOS) – Verses, explanations, audio.
- **Vedabase** (Android) – ISKCON-based library of Vedic texts.
- **Pocket Vedas** (Android / iOS) – Scriptures and philosophical summaries.
- **Daily Hindu Prayers** (Android / iOS) – Mantras, stotras, and rituals.

Buddhism

Websites:

- Access to Insight – Theravāda suttas and essays.
- SuttaCentral.net – Pali Canon with multilingual access.

Mobile Apps:

- **Insight Timer** (Android / iOS) – Buddhist meditations and talks.
- **Suttas & Parittas** (Android) – Key Pali scriptures with English translations.
- **Buddhify** (Android / iOS) – Mindfulness inspired by Buddhist practice.
- **Sutta Central App** (via website) – Responsive mobile access to canonical texts.

Sikhism

Websites:

- SriGranth.org – Full Guru Granth Sahib with exegesis.
- SikhNet.com – Gurbani, youth resources, and Sikh living.

Mobile Apps:

- **iGranth** (Android / iOS) – Guru Granth Sahib with search and translations.
- **SikhNet Gurbani Media Center** (Android / iOS) – Audio kirtans and lectures.
- **Nitnem Gutka** (Android / iOS) – Daily Sikh prayers with Gurmukhi and translations.

Interfaith & Academic Resources

Websites:

- Sacred Texts Archive – Global religious scriptures.
- ReligionFacts.com – Side-by-side religious comparisons.
- JSTOR.org – Academic articles on religious studies.

- Oxford Reference: Religion – Scholarly definitions and entries.

Mobile Apps:

- **Religions of the World** (Android) – Overview of major faiths with doctrines and practices.
- **Coursera / EdX Apps** – Enroll in interfaith and theology courses from top universities.
- **Wikipedia** (Android / iOS) – Useful for quick reference (use with caution and verify).

⚠ Important Reminder:

AI-generated content may **mimic accuracy** but **lack authenticity**. Always verify through **two or more** trusted sources—especially in spiritual matters.

Appendix B: Glossary of Key Terms

Foundational Terms

- **AI (Artificial Intelligence)**: The simulation of human intelligence by machines. AI enables computers to perform tasks like learning, reasoning, problem-solving, and decision-making.
- **Machine Learning (ML)**: A subfield of AI that enables systems to learn from data and improve over time without being explicitly programmed.
- **Natural Language Processing (NLP)**: The branch of AI that focuses on the interaction between computers and human (natural) language, enabling machines to understand, interpret, and generate human language.
- **Algorithm**: A step-by-step set of rules used by a computer to perform a specific task or solve a problem.

Chatbot-Specific Terminology

- **Chatbot**: A software program that uses AI to simulate human-like conversation through text or speech.
- **Large Language Model (LLM)**: A type of AI trained on vast amounts of text data to generate human-like responses. Examples include GPT (OpenAI), Claude (Anthropic), and Gemini (Google).
- **Prompt**: The input or query given to a chatbot. Good prompts can improve the relevance and quality of the output.
- **Completion/Response**: The output or answer generated by the chatbot in response to a prompt.

- **Hallucination (in AI)**: When an AI generates false, misleading, or fabricated information that sounds plausible.
- **Token**: The basic unit of text (e.g., a word or part of a word) used by language models. The model processes input and output in tokens.
- **Context Window**: The amount of text a model can "remember" in a single interaction. GPT-4, for example, can process thousands of tokens at once.
- **Training Data**: The information (usually vast text corpora) used to teach an AI how language works and what different concepts mean.

Technical Components

- **Transformer**: A deep learning architecture that powers LLMs. It allows models to understand relationships between words in a sequence efficiently.
- **Neural Network**: A system of algorithms modeled after the human brain, enabling AI to learn patterns in data.
- **Fine-Tuning**: The process of adapting a pre-trained language model to perform specific tasks or serve a specific audience by training it on additional data.
- **Embedding**: A numerical representation of text used by AI to understand context, meaning, and relationships between words.
- **Pre-trained Model**: A model already trained on a large corpus of data before being used or fine-tuned for specific applications.

Interaction Modes

- **Conversational AI**: AI systems designed for interactive human dialogue, simulating multi-turn conversations with context retention.
- **Multi-turn Conversation**: A dialogue with several back-and-forth exchanges, where the chatbot remembers earlier parts of the conversation.
- **Context Retention**: The model's ability to remember previous messages or topics within a session.
- **Voice Assistant**: A chatbot that uses voice input and output, like Siri, Alexa, or Google Assistant.

Usage & Deployment

- **API (Application Programming Interface)**: A tool that allows developers to connect their applications with AI models for chatbot integration.
- **Inference**: The process of using a trained model to make predictions or generate responses.
- **Latency**: The delay between user input and AI response. Lower latency means faster replies.
- **Chatbot Platform**: A service that hosts chatbots and provides interfaces to use them (e.g., OpenAI, Google Bard, Microsoft Copilot).

Ethics & Safety

- **Bias in AI**: The presence of unfair or unbalanced representations in AI outputs, often due to biased training data.

- **Content Moderation**: Filtering or adjusting chatbot output to remove harmful, offensive, or inappropriate content.
- **Alignment**: Efforts to ensure that AI systems behave in ways aligned with human values, ethics, and goals.
- **Verification**: The process of confirming the accuracy of chatbot output, especially in sensitive areas like religion or science.
- **Transparency**: The clarity about how AI systems function, make decisions, and generate content.

AI Development Concepts

- **Open-source Model**: An AI system whose code and architecture are publicly available, allowing for community development and modification (e.g., Mistral, LLaMA).
- **Closed-source Model**: A proprietary AI system whose internal mechanics are not publicly disclosed (e.g., GPT-4, Claude).
- **Retrieval-Augmented Generation (RAG)**: A hybrid system that enhances chatbot answers by retrieving information from external databases in real time.
- **Memory**: The AI's capability to recall past interactions beyond a single session. Some models (like Claude) have longer memory capacity.

Specialized Applications

- **AI Writing Assistant**: Tools like ChatGPT or Jasper that help users generate text for articles, books, or scripts.
- **Search-Based Chatbots**: Tools like Perplexity AI that combine chatbot functions with real-time web search for accurate citations.

- **AI Ethics**: The study and practice of ensuring that AI systems are designed and used in morally responsible ways.
- **Digital Assistant vs Chatbot**: A digital assistant (e.g., Copilot) is often task-oriented (e.g., scheduling), while a chatbot focuses on conversation and knowledge exchange.

Appendix C: Chatbots and Their Wise Use

(Your Practical Guide to Navigating the Age of Conversational AI)

1. What is a Chatbot?

A chatbot is a computer program powered by artificial intelligence (AI) that simulates conversation with human users, either through text or voice. It can answer questions, provide explanations, generate content, assist with research, or perform various tasks.

Some popular chatbots include:

- **ChatGPT (OpenAI)**
- **Claude (Anthropic)**
- **Gemini (Google)**
- **Copilot (Microsoft)**
- **Perplexity AI**
- **DeepSeek**
- **Mistral-based open-source models**

These tools are available through websites, mobile apps, or integrated into other platforms.

---

2. How Do They Work?

Chatbots are trained using large volumes of text data. They don't understand language like humans do, but predict the most appropriate response based on learned patterns.

Key Concepts:

- **Prompt**: Your question or instruction to the chatbot.
- **Response**: The AI's generated reply.
- **Context**: Information remembered during a session to maintain coherence.
- **Token Limit**: The amount of text the chatbot can process at once.

---

3. How to Use a Chatbot Wisely — Step by Step

This section serves as a practical usage guide for readers.

Step 1: Choose the Right Chatbot

Not all chatbots excel in the same areas. Choose according to your need:

Purpose	Recommended Chatbot
Writing assistance	ChatGPT (GPT-4)
Factual, real-time info	Perplexity AI, Bing Chat
Creative brainstorming	Claude, Gemini
Productivity and coding	Copilot, DeepSeek

Step 2: Write a Clear Prompt

A precise question results in a more accurate answer.

✓ Do:

"Summarize the difference between Sunni and Shia beliefs in under 150 words."

✗ **Avoid vague questions:**

"Tell me about Islam." (Too broad)

Step 3: Check the Sources

Most chatbots do not cite their sources unless specifically built to do so. For religious, medical, or legal topics, always cross-verify with authentic resources such as:

- Quran.com
- Sunnah.com
- IslamQA.info
- SeekersGuidance.org
- Official fatwa portals or university websites

Step 4: Beware of "AI Hallucination"

Chatbots can sometimes generate incorrect or fabricated information with confidence. This is known as an "AI hallucination."

Important: Never rely on AI-generated responses for religious rulings or scholarly conclusions without verification.

Step 5: Know When to Stop

AI is a tool—not a replacement for human reasoning, experience, or spiritual insight. Use it wisely, and with intention.

---

4. Tips for Using Chatbots Effectively in Daily Life

Use Case	How to Use Chatbots Wisely
Religious studies	Ask for summaries or context—always verify with primary sources
Language learning	Practice vocabulary, grammar, and simple conversations
Research and writing	Generate outlines, get feedback, or improve phrasing
Brainstorming	Explore different angles, ideas, and perspectives
Creative projects	Co-create poems, scripts, or stories—but maintain authorship

---

5. Do's and Don'ts of Using Chatbots for Religious Knowledge

✓ DO:

- Use AI for learning and understanding—never for final judgments.
- Ask AI to clarify verses, summarize differences, or explain historical contexts.
- Always compare AI answers with scholarly sources.
- Be curious, but stay cautious.

✗ DON'T:

- Issue fatwas or religious rulings based on chatbot answers.
- Ask AI to "decide" between theological viewpoints.

- Accept uncited information as truth.
- Assume AI is free from bias—it reflects its data and design.

---

6. The Golden Rule: Human Intellect First, AI Second

AI is a tool, not a teacher. It can enhance your understanding and speed up your learning—but it must never replace your conscience, research, or reasoning.

Wisdom, sincerity, and humility remain essential.

Final Thought

Just as a knife can be used to prepare nourishing meals or to harm, chatbots too can be instruments of either clarity or confusion. The difference lies not in the tool—but in the user.

Use AI with humility, verify with knowledge, and walk the path of learning with a heart open to truth.

Appendix D: Types of Errors AI May Encounter in Religious Content Generation

---

1. Misquotation of Sacred Texts

- AI may generate **inaccurate or fabricated verses**, often resembling the real ones but altered in wording or meaning.
- It might **attribute sayings or concepts** to holy books or prophets that don't exist in any authentic source.

2. Out-of-Context Interpretations

- AI may **lift verses or excerpts without context**, leading to distorted meanings.
- Lacks understanding of **historical, linguistic, and theological background** essential for proper interpretation.

3. Conflating Different Religions

- AI can **merge teachings** from multiple faiths inappropriately, presenting them as part of a single tradition.
- It may **confuse terminologies**, rituals, or theological concepts due to overlapping language.

4. Inaccurate Attribution

- Assigns quotes to the **wrong book, or religious leader**.
- Commonly confuses **hadiths with Quranic verses**, or **Talmudic laws with Biblical commands**, etc.

5. Simplification of Complex Theology

- Reduces rich theological debates into **over-simplified or binary explanations**.

- Misses out on **nuances**, such as differences between sects, schools of thought, or denominations.

6. Invented or Non-Existent Sources

- AI may reference **books, scholars, or traditions that do not exist**, because it fills gaps with statistically probable phrases rather than verified facts.

7. Misrepresentation of Religious Laws

- Generates **incomplete, outdated, or incorrect rulings** in matters like worship, ethics, diet, marriage, or finance.
- Lacks the authority and **jurisprudential methodology (fiqh, halakha, canon law, etc.)** to make such judgments.

8. Cultural Bias or Secular Framing

- AI often reflects **Western academic or secular interpretations**, which may dilute or misrepresent the **faith-based worldview** of religious adherents.
- May **frame religion as a sociological phenomenon** rather than a divine truth system.

9. Contradictory Answers

- Due to inconsistent training data, AI may provide **conflicting responses** to the same question at different times.
- May **affirm and deny the same theological principle** without clarity.

10. Lack of Moral or Spiritual Insight

- AI lacks **empathy, spirituality, or moral compass**—it cannot feel reverence or grasp the soul of sacred teachings.
- May respond in ways that are **disrespectful, insensitive, or even offensive** without recognizing it.

Appendix E: Recommended Resources on AI Chatbots, Their Uses, and Ethical Concerns

---

Books

1. **"Artificial Intelligence: A Guide for Thinking Humans"** by Melanie Mitchell
    - A readable and critical overview of how AI works and its current limitations.
2. **"Weapons of Math Destruction"** by Cathy O'Neil
    - Explores how AI and algorithms can amplify bias and injustice.
3. **"Talking to Robots: Tales from Our Human-Robot Futures"** by David Ewing Duncan
    - A creative look at how AI and chatbots may shape different areas of human life.
4. **"Ethics of Artificial Intelligence and Robotics"** (Stanford Encyclopedia of Philosophy, online entry)
    - A comprehensive academic resource.
5. **"The Alignment Problem: Machine Learning and Human Values"** by Brian Christian
    - Investigates how to align AI behavior with human ethics.
6. **"Rebooting AI: Building Artificial Intelligence We Can Trust"** by Gary Marcus and Ernest Davis
    - Focuses on why current AI (including chatbots) falls short of true intelligence.

◆ Academic Journals & Articles

1. **AI & Society** (Springer)
    - Covers social implications and ethical aspects of AI technologies.
2. **Journal of Artificial Intelligence Research (JAIR)**
    - Peer-reviewed research, including foundational and ethical discussions.
3. **Nature Machine Intelligence**
    - High-quality articles on AI's development, applications, and concerns.
4. **Ethics and Information Technology** (Springer)
    - Focuses specifically on the ethical issues in emerging technologies.
5. **ACM Transactions on Human-Robot Interaction (THRI)**
    - Relevant for chatbot and conversational AI research.

◆ Websites and Platforms

1. **Stanford HAI (Human-Centered Artificial Intelligence)**
   🔗 hai.stanford.edu
    - Balancing AI advancement with ethical responsibility.
2. **AI Now Institute**
   🔗 ainowinstitute.org
    - Leading research on social implications of AI technologies.
3. **OpenAI Blog**
   🔗 openai.com/blog

- Official blog on how tools like ChatGPT are developed and their limitations.

4. **Partnership on AI**

   🔗 partnershiponai.org

   - A global initiative focused on responsible AI.

5. **Future of Life Institute**

   🔗 futureoflife.org

   - Explores long-term impacts and ethics of AI.

6. **MIT Technology Review – AI Section**

   🔗 technologyreview.com

   - Popular science and tech publication covering AI developments.

7. **AI Ethics Lab**

   🔗 aiethicslab.com

   - Bridging ethics and practice in real-world AI applications.

◆ Bonus: Courses & Guides

- **Elements of AI**

  🔗 elementsofai.com

  - A free, beginner-friendly course on how AI works and its implications.

- **Google's AI Ethics Guidelines**

  🔗 ai.google/responsibilities/responsible-ai-practices

  - A corporate perspective on AI responsibility.

Appendix F: Comparative List of Major AI Chatbots

Chatbot	Developer	Strengths	Ideal For	Limitations	Free Version?
ChatGPT (GPT-4)	OpenAI	Highly creative, great language fluency, memory in Pro version	Writing, education, brainstorming, code help	GPT-4 only available in paid tier	✓ (GPT-3.5)
Claude (3.0)	Anthropic	Long context window (great for large files), polite tone	Document summarization, thoughtful analysis	Not always concise or assertive	✓

Gemini (Pro 1.5)	Google (DeepMind)	Integrated with Google services, rich multimedia answers	Search-integrated tasks, research help	Some answers lack depth; regional restrictions	✓
Microsoft Copilot	Microsoft + OpenAI	Seamless Office/Edge integration, productivity tools	MS Word, Excel, Outlook support, summaries	Limited use outside Microsoft ecosystem	✓
Perplexity AI	Perplexity.ai	Real-time citations, always shows sources	Research, fact-checking, verifying information	Short responses; less nuanced generation	✓
DeepSeek Chat	DeepSeek AI (China)	Math, coding, reasoning, multilingual input	Technical and STEM-related queries	UI still evolving; fewer creative capabilities	✓

Mistral-based Bots	Various platforms	Open-source, fast, lightweight, customizable	Developers, hobbyists, secure local use	Requires setup; not beginner-friendly	✓ (varies)

Legend:

- **✓ Free Version?** Indicates whether a version of the chatbot is available without payment.
- **Memory in Pro**: Indicates that the chatbot remembers context within and across chats, but only in the Pro version.
- **Multilingual**: Most support multiple languages, but fluency and accuracy vary.

Tips for Choosing the Right Chatbot:

Task	Best Chatbot(s)
Writing and editing	ChatGPT, Claude
Real-time factual research	Perplexity AI, Gemini
Summarizing long documents	Claude, DeepSeek
Coding help	ChatGPT, Copilot, DeepSeek
Working within Microsoft Office	Copilot

Task	Best Chatbot(s)
Handling large file inputs	Claude
Privacy-focused or offline use	Mistral-based bots

Note: These tools are evolving rapidly. Feature updates may occur frequently. Always check the official site for the latest capabilities and access options.

About the Author

Iftikhar Ahmad is an Assistant Professor with over 22 years of distinguished experience in teaching and research. Holding a Master's degree in Physics (M.Sc. Physics), his academic journey is defined by a passion for exploring the intersection of Islamic teachings and modern scientific principles. His research is grounded in intellectual curiosity, driven by a commitment to showcasing the timeless relevance of Islam in the contemporary world.

Academic and Professional Background

Iftikhar Ahmad's academic path began with a deep passion for the natural sciences, which led him to pursue his Master's degree in Physics. This rigorous training provided the foundation for his interdisciplinary research, particularly the integration of Islamic thought with modern scientific discovery. Over two decades of teaching, he has mentored students in both the sciences and humanities, fostering critical thinking and a deeper understanding of the world.

As an Assistant Professor, he is committed to nurturing intellectual integrity and empowering his students to think independently and critically, while encouraging them to explore the connections between science, philosophy, and spirituality.

Research and Scholarly Contributions

In addition to his teaching, Iftikhar Ahmad is renowned for his research on the modern interpretation of Quranic verses, especially in the context of contemporary scientific developments. His work bridges the gap between traditional Islamic scholarship and modern science, examining the Quran from multidisciplinary perspectives such as physics, biology, sociology, and psychology.

He explores how the Quran offers a comprehensive framework for understanding the universe, humanity's place in it, and the challenges facing modern society. His research seeks to demonstrate that Islam is not just a spiritual guide but a practical and intellectual framework for addressing the complexities of the modern world.

Intellectual Approach

Iftikhar Ahmad's intellectual approach combines a commitment to objectivity with a deep respect for Islamic tradition. While his work remains rooted in the faith, he maintains an academic distance, ensuring that his research remains rigorous, impartial, and accessible to a broad audience. His studies address both religious and scientific questions with an emphasis on intellectual clarity and relevance to contemporary issues.

This intellectual rigor enables his work to transcend the boundaries of traditional scholarship, offering new insights into how Islamic principles can be applied to modern challenges, particularly in the realm of science and technology.

Philosophy of Writing

At the core of Iftikhar Ahmad's writing lies the belief in the harmony between science and faith. He argues that Islam, as a comprehensive system of life, provides profound insights into the workings of the universe and the nature of human existence. His writings aim to demonstrate that the Quran's teachings are not just a spiritual guide but a complete framework for understanding the world, offering solutions to many of the challenges faced by modern society.

By combining scientific knowledge with Islamic wisdom, Iftikhar Ahmad's work inspires readers to appreciate the holistic nature of Islam and its relevance to contemporary life.

Personal Interests

Outside of academia, Iftikhar Ahmad is deeply committed to the comparative study of Islam and science. He is particularly interested in exploring how Islamic teachings can guide humanity through the rapid technological and social changes of the modern world. His ongoing research examines the dynamic relationship between traditional Islamic scholarship and contemporary scientific understanding, reinforcing the concept that Islam offers timeless guidance for all aspects of life.

Residing in Pakistan, he continues to teach, write, and engage in intellectual discourse, contributing to a deeper understanding of the intersection between Islam and modern scientific knowledge.

Present and Upcoming Works: A Journey of Intellectual and Spiritual Exploration

As Iftikhar Ahmad continues exploring the intersection of Islamic teachings and modern sciences, several forthcoming projects are going to have a significant impact in both academic and religious circles. These works are designed to further strengthen the intellectual foundation of Islam as a timeless and comprehensive system, offering robust rebuttals to misconceptions, a deeper understanding of the Prophet Muhammad (PBUH), and a detailed analysis of the Quran's relationship with modern science. Below is a brief introduction to each of these projects:

PUBLISHED BOOKS

1. **"Parenting in the Modern Age: Insights from Islam"**

   In today's rapidly changing world, raising children presents complex challenges. This book draws on Islamic principles to offer practical guidance on nurturing responsible, compassionate, and wise individuals. It emphasizes timeless values like justice, empathy, and balance, providing a unique approach to modern parenting.

2. **"Religious Content in the Age of AI"**

   A groundbreaking intellectual exploration that delves into the mechanisms of artificial intelligence and its impact on religious content. This book meticulously examines the types of mistakes AI makes when handling sacred teachings, offering actionable solutions for developers and a call to action for religious authorities. With deep, unbiased research, it provides a thorough analysis of how we can responsibly integrate technology without compromising the sanctity of religious knowledge. A unique work that addresses a critical issue in the digital age with clarity and depth.

3. **"The Swings of Gender Roles"**

   The author thoughtfully explores the shifting landscape of gender roles, tracing their evolution through history, science, philosophy, and religion. In response to the current climate of confusion and polarization around gender, this book offers a balanced, reflective perspective. Grounded in Islamic wisdom, it delves into the impacts of extreme views—both traditional and modern—on society, while offering a harmonious model that honors the distinct roles of men and women. With a focus on clarity and insight, this book invites readers from all walks of life to engage with an intellectually honest, thoughtful conversation on gender and its place in the world today.

4. **"Tiny Shifts Big Relief"**

   It is a microbook that explores how small, manageable changes can lead to lasting emotional clarity and mental ease. In a world that often demands big transformations, this book offers a gentler path—through practical, tiny steps that reduce stress, burnout, and procrastination. Each short topic presents one powerful shift designed to help you feel more in control. Whether you're overwhelmed, stuck, or simply seeking simplicity, this is a guide to progress without pressure. Real change doesn't have to be dramatic—it just needs to begin.

5. **"The Pain of Being Wrong"**

   It is a poetic-prose microbook that explores what it means to live with failure, regret, and emotional invisibility. It tells the story of being misunderstood, unheard, and carrying a burden no one else can see. Through short reflections called "echoes," the book captures the quiet pain of inner struggle. It is not a guide to healing—but a companion for those who've known silence more intimately than words. A voice for those who've lived between apology and hope.

6. **"W.O.M.A.N."**

   It is a groundbreaking exploration of womanhood through the timeless values of **Wisdom, Offering, Modesty, Authority, and Nobility**. Blending history, theology, psychology, and global gender discourse, it challenges both modern stereotypes and inherited misconceptions. This book doesn't offer slogans—it offers depth. It invites readers beyond the noise of ideology into a richer, spiritually grounded vision of feminine dignity. For those seeking clarity, not conformity, *W.O.M.A.N.* is a mirror—subtle, strong, and unapologetically true.

7. **"Hybrid Hearts"**

   It is a genre-defying exploration of authorship, creativity, and the silent revolutions sparked by artificial intelligence. Part memoir, part manifesto, it reflects what happens when human vulnerability meets digital precision—not to compete, but to co-create. This book doesn't debate technology—it reveals what the machine exposes in us. Structured around five creative "revolts," it speaks to writers, artists, and seekers grappling with change, ego, and meaning. At its heart, *Hybrid Hearts* is a story about transformation—when the mirror writes back.

8. **"Muhammad, A Real Role Model for Humanity"**

   This book offers a comprehensive and deeply respectful exploration of the life of Prophet Muhammad (peace be upon him). Moving beyond surface narratives, this book examines every dimension of his life—personal, family, professional, prophetic, political, economic, and administrative—with intellectual rigor and utmost authenticity. It addresses both well-known and lesser-discussed aspects of his journey, carefully clarifying areas where misconceptions have taken root due to lack of knowledge. Through unmatched depth and precision, this book stands as a unique historical study, bringing to light the timeless greatness of the most influential and revered human being in history.

9. **"The Philosophy of Sin"**

   A single-volume exploration of one of humanity's most loaded and misunderstood concepts. Bridging philosophy, psychology, neuroscience, and Islamic thought, it re-examines sin not as dogma, but as a moral signal guiding conscience and compassion. Beyond judgment or denial, this work offers a balanced, humane reflection on guilt, justice, mercy, and modern digital shame. A thoughtful invitation to rediscover what sin truly means — and why, even today, it might still matter.

NEXT COMING BOOKS

10. **"The Solution Series: A Modern Approach in the Light of Islam"**

    It is a six-volume exploration of today's most pressing global challenges—ranging from economic inequality and racism to gender ethics, youth crises, mental health, and technological dilemmas. Rooted in both timeless Islamic wisdom and contemporary interdisciplinary analysis, each volume offers a balanced, practical, and spiritually grounded response to modern complexities. This series bridges revelation with reality, guiding readers toward clarity, justice, and resilience in a fragmented world.

11. **"Why Islam? An Intellectually Rigorous Exploration of History, Other Faiths and Modern Sciences."**

This work undertakes a comprehensive, comparative analysis of Islam alongside other contemporary worldviews, highlighting its enduring relevance through an objective yet scholarly examination of history, diverse faith traditions, and modern scientific insights. Rather than presenting Islam solely as a set of religious rituals, the book explores it as a holistic way of life capable of meeting the intellectual, moral, and social challenges of humanity. This book offers a thoughtful and evidence-based argument for why Islam provides the most balanced and effective framework for addressing the complex issues confronting the world today.

12. **"The Quran and the Sciences: An Encyclopedia of Divine Wisdom and Modern Knowledge."**

This groundbreaking project stands as a monumental contribution to the Comparative study of the Quran and contemporary sciences. Spanning over 6000 pages, this multi-volume work offers an in-depth analysis of more than 1,000 Quranic verses, presenting modern interpretations that align with verified scientific knowledge. Rooted in fundamental Islamic sources and authentic scientific theories, it represents an unparalleled achievement in Islamic scholarship. Designed as a critical academic resource, this work aspires to shape the curriculum of leading universities worldwide, reaffirming the Quran's timeless relevance and intellectual depth.

These upcoming works are not only a continuation of the author's lifelong intellectual journey but also a call for readers to rediscover the profound harmony between faith and reason, the past and the present, the sacred and the scientific. Each project serves as a milestone in presenting a holistic, scientifically grounded, and philosophically rich understanding of Islam's timeless relevance in the modern world. Through these efforts, he aspires to ignite deeper reflection, foster meaningful dialogue, and unveil the universal truths that Islam offers to guide and uplift every dimension of human life.

Call to Action: Securing the Future of Religious Knowledge

We are at a pivotal moment in history, where the wisdom of sacred traditions intersects with the digital intelligence of machines. The question is not whether artificial intelligence will influence religious knowledge, but how deeply it will shape what generations have preserved through study, reverence, and devotion.

This book is not merely a cautionary tale — it is a call to action, a reminder to every individual who values truth over convenience, reverence over automation, and faith over misinformation.

Preserving the integrity of religious knowledge is not solely the responsibility of scholars. It is a collective trust — an amanah — for all of humanity.

To Religious Leaders and Scholars:

Your voice has never been more crucial. In this algorithm-driven era, you are the guardians of authenticity. If you remain passive, others — machines and misinformed voices — will fill the void. Speak. Write. Engage. Collaborate with technologists. Bring the light of classical wisdom into the digital spaces where millions now seek guidance.

You are not just spiritual leaders — you are the protectors of truth in an age where it is at risk of being diluted.

To Technologists and AI Developers:

What you build will influence the spiritual future of humanity. Code with conscience. Build with reverence. Consult scholars. Respect sacred texts. Every algorithm carries the potential for bias, shaped by the data it learns from. Will your creations uphold truth, or perpetuate errors?

You are not simply crafting tools — you are shaping the spiritual landscape for generations to come.

To Every Reader, Seeker, and User:

You have more power than you realize. With each click, share, and search, you either help protect sacred knowledge or contribute to its distortion. Before forwarding that quote or accepting an AI-generated answer, pause. Verify. Ask. Learn.

Truth is not viral. Truth is verified.

Be the voice that protects authenticity. Be the guardian who questions what is synthetic.

The Time to Act Is Now. The Responsibility Is Ours.

The digital tide is rising. Misinformation is becoming the norm. But as long as there are hearts dedicated to protecting truth, hope remains.

Let this book not be an endpoint but the beginning of a movement:

- A movement of conscious users.
- A movement of responsible developers.
- A movement of awakened scholars.
- A movement of individuals who understand that machines may replicate information — but never revelation.

Let us rise as guardians, not just of tradition, but of truth.

Together, let us ensure that what is sacred remains sacred — now and always.

Golden Rule of Intellectual Integrity:

"No convenience is worth the cost of truthfulness and authenticity."

— Iftikhar Ahmad

Author, Researcher, and Witness to the Crossroads of Revelation and Code

www.ingramcontent.com/pod-product-compliance
Lightning Source LLC
LaVergne TN
LVHW022052200926
848481LV00003B/884
* 9 7 9 8 2 2 7 8 1 3 0 9 1 *